The Love Of My Life

THE LOVE OF MY LIFE

A Family's True Story of
a Father and Husband's Battle
with Alzheimer's

Patricia Michaud

The Love of my Life.
Copyright © 2016, 2022 by Patricia Michaud.

Second Edition.

First originally published by Page Publishing, Inc. (2016)

All rights reserved. No part of this book may be reproduced in any form or by any electronic or mechanical means, including information storage and retrieval systems, without permission in writing from the publisher and author, except by reviewers, who may quote brief passages in a review.

This publication contains the opinions and ideas of its author. It is intended to provide helpful and informative material on the subjects addressed in the publication. The authors and publisher specifically disclaim all responsibility for any liability, loss, or risk, personal or otherwise, which is incurred as a consequence, directly or indirectly, of the use and application of any of the contents of this book.

Certain stock imagery © Shutterstock.com.

ISBN: 978-1-63950-149-6   [Paperback Edition]
        978-1-63950-150-2   [eBook Edition]

Printed and bound in The United States of America.

Writers Apex

Gateway Towards Success

1309 Coffeen Avenue
STE 1200, Sheridan,
Wyoming, 82801 USA
+13179780258
www.writersapex.com

To my beloved husband, who put up such a courageous fight for such a long time. Thank you for being the person you were. To Cortney, my oldest daughter and my two grandsons, Gage and JW. Thank you for always being there with the challenges we've been through. I would like to thank my family and friends for all their support. To Dr. Joseph Quinn, Joe's doctor. To my counselor, Shirley Price, for all their help. To Mary Karr, who is my comrade in rms who went through the same things as I did.

We need to continue to fight and conquer this wretched disease, Alzheimer's.

My Parents

Your love is strong and was never meek
You said your vows, promise and keep
His heart was big, your love so true
Through thick and thin, you've made it through
All the bitter ends may seem hard to take
It's your eternal love that will never break

I love you,

Cortney Turner

CONTENTS

Chapter 1: Let's Start at the Beginning 11
Chapter 2: The Fun Begins in the Year 2001 16
Chapter 3: The Appointment and Diagnosis 20
Chapter 4: Becoming a Full-Time Caregiver 29
Chapter 5: Thank You, God 56
Chapter 6: Celebration of Life Party 58
Chapter 7: Joe Moves into a Care Facility 60
Chapter 8: Downward Spiral, April 2013 72
Chapter 9: Ross's Diagnosis 88
Chapter 10: Thoughts on My Brothers 96
Chapter 11: What, Parkinson's Too? 99
Chapter 12: How to Say Good-bye 104
Chapter 13: Who Am I Now? 113
Chapter 14: Eulogy to Joe 117
Chapter 15: Prayers and Poems That Comfort Me 125
Chapter 16: What Helped Me Out 140
Chapter 17: A Recap 145

Why I Needed To Write This Book

This book is about my husband, Joe, and our daughter's father, who was diagnosed first with mild cognitive impairment (the onset of Alzheimer's) in 2003 at the age of fifty-six. Then by the age of sixty, he had full-blown Alzheimer's. Joe has been in a study program since the first with Dr. Quinn at the Oregon Health Sciences University (OHSU).

This book is to help you with preparing, to give you knowledge about, and how to cope with what Alzheimer's throws at you and your family.

Why I wrote this book is a big question. I didn't know a thing about the disease. Hell, I didn't know the name mild cognitive impairment, let alone the word Alzheimer's. But let me tell you now, I may not be an expert, but I can sure help you out if you need any questions answered.

You need to know what life-changing experiences you will be going through. This book will tell you about all kinds of other books, seminars, and classes. But what those books don't tell you are the things that go on in your home and in your life with your loved ones. That is what I wanted to do in this book, to give you a better insight of what goes on and how it changes you and your family.

First, there are signs to look for:

1. Having them always say that you didn't tell them something and then getting mad at you because of it.
2. Written or verbally understanding.
3. Repeating themselves.
4. Difficulty completing tasks at home.

5. Having problems communicating with friends and family.
6. Getting upset with themselves because they cannot find things, and they just don't understand.
7. Problems remembering names.
8. Misplacing items.
9. Getting lost.
10. Having problems at home.
11. Difficulty performing familiar tasks.

All this is nerve breaking and gut wrenching to see your loved one go through.

This disease is like no other disease you would know about. Cancer, leukemia, multiple sclerosis, Parkinson's disease are all horrible diseases. But with Alzheimer's, it will strip you of yourself, your knowledge of being any type of normal human being. I'll tell you more as we go along.

In an article by the *Oregonian*, by Julie Sullivan and the Alzheimer's Association, it states a report warns that Alzheimer's will be the "defining disease" of the baby boomers, with one in eight eventually developing the progressive brain disorder. About ten million boomers can expect to develop the disease, and there is no prevention or cure as of today.

Right now, just in Oregon, where I live, there are about seventy thousand that have Alzheimer's, and by the year 2030, there will be about seventy-six million people living with this dreadful disease called Alzheimer's. Eventually, it will go higher because when all the baby boomers get to sixty-five or so. We do not understand what this life-changing disease can do to us.

If you become a caregiver or know someone who is a caregiver, God bless you and thank you for all your hard work. If you know someone who is taking care of someone with Alzheimer's, get them the help they need, because it is a long, hard road to go by yourself.

I can definitely say that from experience. You think that you can go at it alone, and maybe you can at first, but it is so hard, physically and mentally draining. The longer you are into it, the harder it gets. You need to have your family and your core group around you.

CHAPTER 1

Let's Start at the Beginning

Joe was born in Portland, Oregon, in 1947. He is the oldest of the three brothers, Ross is six years younger, and Tony is the baby of the family; he is nine years younger. When Joe was sixteen, his mom passed away from bone cancer. It was hard on the entire family, so Joe's dad remarried shortly after to help bring up three boys.

At the age of eighteen, Joe joined the Navy as a radio man. With a knowledge of electronics and having been a part of the amateur radio FFC for four years prior, it helped secure his position in the service. He was stationed at Kodiak, Alaska, and then at Navcommsta, Cam Ranh Bay, Vietnam.

In 1969, Joe had served his four years and was honorably discharged in 1972. At that time, I was living with my roommate, Carol. One Friday night, she and her boyfriend suggested that I go to a party with them. It was an after-hours party that started at 1:00 a.m. Who in their right mind would like to go to a party that starts at 1:00 a.m.? Considering that you have been up at 5:00 a.m. to go to work that day. But I did it for Carol's sake because she had been telling me all the stories of this guy whom she had been skiing with named Joe, together with Jim, for the winter. And she kept telling me that she had the perfect guy for me, and boy, was she right.

Well, I did go after being scolded about not getting out a lot—though I was already seeing a person from work that no one new about—so I decided to go (what the heck), and look what happened.

As I sat and people-watched, Joe started watching me and decided he should make the first move.

He came over and sat down beside me. My first thought was that I was not interested. But Carol said he was a great guy, so I gave him a chance.

So Joe and I started dating that next day. From that first date, we were inseparable. We also knew that we were going to be married within the first two weeks. He would always say to me, "Life is no bed of roses." I knew he had to be sure.

It took him about ten months before he would ask me. Well, he truly didn't really ask me to marry him. But he did show me the ring. I said it was about time, kissed him, and off I went to show all my neighbors, who loved him like I did; they always kept asking me, "When is he going to propose to you?"

Joe was one of those people that you or everyone could feel so comfortable being around and talking to. That your life history would jumped right out of you when you were talking to him without really thinking about it. He could make you feel so at ease and relaxed.

Because my mom always watched my back, as mothers tend to do, she was a little wary of Joe since our relationship was moving along somewhat quickly for a mother's standards.

At that time, my parents were out of town when Joe and I met. It was going to be about three weeks before they got back into Portland, so I kept calling her to tell her everything that what was going on.

You have to remember, I had just turned twenty-one when I met Joe. I didn't have a lot of dating experience at all.

Mom called me one night to say that when she got home, she would like to have a long talk with him, just to see what type of gentleman he was. I told him about my concerns with her. He looked at me and smiled and told me not to worry; he would be happy to talk to her.

I introduced them to each other, and off they went to the backyard to have the talk with Joe to learn of his future intentions. My mom said to me that night, Joe was either a damn good liar or a damn good salesman; she didn't know which one yet. A belief she kept for years.

With Joe, what you see is what you get: a kind and loving person. After that, I thought my mom loved Joe more than she loved me sometimes.

One day, my roommate, Carol, told me she was going to be moving in with her boyfriend. I told Joe that I couldn't afford to be on my own. Joe asked me if I got along with my parents. I said, "Sure I do." So we suggested that I should move back home to save money, and within a few months, Joe moved into a little playhouse on my parents' property. We knew we were going to be getting married the next year anyway.

September 21, 1973, was our wedding day. My father was a man who hardly ever showed much emotion, but he could not keep the smile from his face. I kept asking him, "Are you just happy to get rid of me, or what?" All I knew that day was my life had truly begun. And what a honeymoon we had planned. We traveled up to Canada then drove through it till we got to the top of Montana, and down we started heading for home. What a great honeymoon, two weeks of enjoyment. We started to make many plans, from buying a home, to having children, to what kind of traveling we would like to do, and what countries we would like to go see, all the backpacking and camping trips we were planning to do, even where our lives would take us in our old age. We couldn't wait for some of our retirement venture that we wanted to do.

One year after we purchased our home, our first daughter, Cortney, was born. Then twenty-one months later, our youngest daughter, Morgan, was born. Both times, before the girls were born, Joe was working in management, and the company he worked for was having labor problems; in other words, the company employees were striking. Because he had the ability to work from home and not cross the picket lines, as he worked, he could watch television, and he heard the names and decided that those were the names of the girls. Cortney was an actress on a talk show, Morgan being a role of a female ranger. After discussing the first names, I came up with their middle names, Cortney Anne and Morgan Marie.

As a dad, Joe was playful yet stern. He believed in rules and responsibility and also that a church was the place for families every Sunday. He trusted his gut and would let me take the lead in raising the girls but would lay down the law when need be. He was fair to them. As he was the only male in the house, he had to deal with a lot of emotional females.

He once said that when the girls were old enough to date that he would leave and not come back until they were married. He was devoted to making sure that they were strong enough to stand up for themselves. Additionally, he showed them how to do activities that boys mostly learned: how to throw a football, pitch a tent, and even gut a fish, since Joe was a fly-fisherman and loved to tie his own flies and make his fishing reel. On our outing, we would even pick up the roadkill on the side of the road so he could use the fur for the feathers. It got to be a game for the girls to yell "Roadkill!" when they was something. What fun we had.

Our summers were packed full of camping trips and sightseeing. We would pack up the car and leave, heading in any direction just to see where we ended up. We had annual camping trips with the ham radio club and our yearly trips to Beverly Beach or the Metolius River or Fort Stevens to camp as a family. We took several trips up to Banff, Canada, too. My mom would go with us after my dad passed away, and Joe was always happy to have her with us.

Sometimes, Joe would call me on Friday nights from work to tell me to pack up the girls. He would get home from work about 5:00 p.m. And off we would go for a drive to the river or up to the mountains to have a barbecue and play in the water somewhere. One of Joe's favorite sayings to Cortney was "We are sightseeing!" which really meant, "We are lost, but don't worry, it will be fine."

While "sightseeing," he liked to pay a little too much attention to the scenery instead of the road. There were a few times that he came close to driving us off the road because he was watching a herd of elk or a gathering of geese or a big semitruck full of livestock.

Joe was a very smart man. He also took so much pride in everything he did, which made him a great husband and father and employee too.

THE LOVE OF MY LIFE

He worked for Fred Meyer for over thirty-seven years as a senior programmer analyst. We had our whole life ahead of us. We had retirement plans up and running. We knew where we were going and looking forward to it. We were starting to expand our family, with our oldest having her own children. Grandchildren are a blessed event, and life was looking good. We never lacked for entertainment as the Michaud family.

From his side to my side of the family, there are a lot of us, and boy were we a loud and playful bunch of big kids all the time. But Joe was always the head of the family to each and every one of us, right down to the nieces and nephews. Even our good friends knew who to go to if they ever needed anything.

Our life was on its way, and we were looking forward to it. Just being together, knowing that we would always be with each other. Joe told me when we got married that I was on a fifty-year contract, with the option to renew after that.

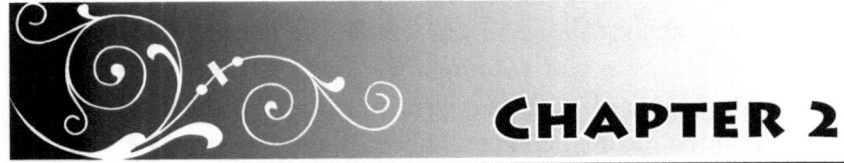

CHAPTER 2

The Fun Begins in the Year 2001

The year was 2001. Boy, what do you say about something that changes your life forever?

To tell this story is going to be so hard for me, because I truly had no idea I would ever be going through something like this in my entire lifetime. And I wish that no one else would have to go through it too.

What do you say after being with one man for over forty-two years, when you take your marriage vows for better or for worse, for richer and poorer, in sickness and health. Sickness, that is such an understatement for what the disease Alzheimer's does to a family.

Yes, we had good times and bad times together, and yes, there were times I could drop-kick him right down a flight of stairs or off a cliff sometimes, but I love him so much and could tell him anything. He was my best friend and lover, the father of our two beautiful daughters, whom he loved so much. We would play and laugh a lot. The girls had to learn growing up that they stood on either side of Joe and me. Because we would always be holding hands with each other. Don't get me wrong, we had some good knock-down drag-out fights too. I was brought up on a block with twelve guys, so I learned how to fight or wrestle. So when we would get into a big fight, we would end up wrestling, which I would always lose because he would pin me down, and then he'd do something or say something to make me laugh.

He would always say something like, "You know that you are so Irish and German, that is why you cannot think fast on your feet. Your brain and your mouth do not want to connect at the same time." (Which is true when I get upset or mad.)

Boy, would that make me madder. Then, he would make me laugh harder by doing something so far off the wall or send me flowers that the fight would be over with.

You just can't stay upset with a person who does things like that to you. I do remember this one fight we got into, where we got into a huge disagreement.

I was so furious one time that I did not speak to him for three days. And that makes it kind of hard when you live together. Joe would also drive me to my work and then drive to his job.

So he just kept sending me flowers to my office and promised he'd call. One day we had a long discussion, and he made me laugh, then everything was back to normal.

Joe and I would always do fun things, like take some classes together. So in 1999, we decided to take a class called CERT (community emergency response team). It was developed for the Department of Homeland Security, Fire Administration Emergency Management Institute.

Because of all of Joe's knowledge in being a ham radio operator, he knew Morse Code and was a great electrician. It couldn't hurt having some knowledge, so in case of a disaster, we would know something. I would also get my ham radio license to help out in case of a disaster, but basically to get everybody off my back, because I would talk on the rig without a license, and Joe would get mad at me and say he would get called by the FCC if I did not stop it.

Joe was beginning to have trouble remembering and forget a lot of things you would say to him, and he would get so mad at you and say that you never told him anything.

Even when people stopped by the house, like one night my brother Martin came by to show us his new pickup, and Joe couldn't remember the color of the pickup when he left. (It was blue.) Or when people would call him on the phone. Lots of little things that would stick in your mind and you know that just isn't right.

I was working for a retail store called Meyer and Frank. I was there for over twelve years. Prior to all this, the company got bought out. So all the upper management personnel got laid off in 2001. During that time, I could see things starting to happen with him.

He was still working at Fred Meyer's, a grocery/apparel/hardware store. The tagline for the store was "One-Stop Shopping," and it had everything in the world for sale. Working there for over thirty-seven years, we had a lot of knowledge about everything.

He was becoming stressed with his job because of a corporate merger that was rumored (and inevitably happened). With the possible layoffs that would occur.

Joe would do odd things. He was very argumentative toward me; he would not remember conversations and generally forget and repeat himself.

In 2002, I received a call from the emergency management in Gresham, Oregon, asking me if I would like to go to Atlanta, Georgia, to apply for a job with Homeland Security.

I started my new career with FEMA (Federal Emergency Management Agency). After two weeks in Atlanta, I was deployed to Saraland, Alabama, where I worked in a DRC (disaster recovery center). I was made the manager of the DRC. I loved my job, being there, trying to help all these people who had just gone through a hurricane themselves.

It made me feel like I was accomplishing something in my life at this time. With losing my job and the girls growing up, I needed something that I could call all my own.

I could or would be deployed to areas where different major emergency disasters occurred, like hurricanes and floods and tornadoes, to help give the residents of the area relief and care. This would also mean that I would be out of town and away from Joe for up to three to four months at a time. I didn't worry too much because he was still working and doing good at his job, I thought, as far as I knew.

THE LOVE OF MY LIFE

I also had my daughters to check in on him and help with the dog and cat if he wanted it. I would also call every night to talk to everybody and find out how everybody was doing. The girls did say that their dad was a little off his game, and the house was kind of messy. But besides that, everyone was doing great, and he was still Joe. In the back of my mind, I knew I was going to have to do something, because this just wasn't my husband; he didn't act this way.

CHAPTER 3

The Appointment and Diagnosis

Happier times just before he was diagnosed, with mild cognitive impairment. He was 56, and I was 52 year old.

THE LOVE OF MY LIFE

In early February of 2003, Joe and I took a trip to Las Vegas for a little vacation after Meyer and Frank got bought out by Robinson May company. And I was so looking forward to it. But the plane ride, or just getting on the plane, was a trip in itself. When we were getting on, above the seats was a little sign designating what the aisle was and the seat letter. We were to have seats *A* and *B*. The little sign said "A–C," cutting the letter B to, I don't know, save ink? *The argument between Joe and I was amazing to all the other passengers trying to board, whom we were holding up in the aisle. Joe just refused to sit down because there was no B seat.*

Finally, after a few minutes of heated discussion, I told Joe to sit the hell down and shut the hell up. As the passengers that we held up were passing us, you should have seen the looks they gave us.

When we finally did get to Las Vegas, he was totally out of his element, and it was like I had brought a child on vacation. All in all, we had a great time. We did all the Las Vegas tourist enjoyment. Like walking the Strip during the day to see what going on and then enjoying the nightlife with all the beautiful lights, with a few shows thrown in for good behavior. The sad thing was Joe did not remember some of the things we did, but I will always remember our time in Vegas

Joe lost his job right after we got back from the trip. He was called into a meeting where they thanked him for all his hard work through the years then gave him his pink slip. A year later, when I talked to some of his ex-coworkers, they let me know that they had laid him off because he was having problems remembering things.

Joe was acting so weird and unpredictable before our trip to Las Vegas that I called and made an appointment for him with our family doctor once we got home from our trip. Dr. Smith-Cupani did some testing and couldn't find anything wrong with his physical health but could see his cognitive memory was having trouble.

She referred us to a neurological doctor. It was in February of 2003. All we knew was that this was some kind of memory doctor.

So we had a new appointment to go to with a new doctor by the name of Dr. Reiter, a previous neurological assessment. He said that Joe had shown impaired visual and auditory memory. The test took over two hours, and boy, was he thorough. I sat in the back of the room on a couch while he was being tested.

The first thing that Dr. Reiter asked Joe to do was to remember three words, *penny*, *month*, and *flower*, then asked him to subtract by seven starting from a hundred for as long as he could. He then had Joe draw pictures of certain items and repeat the alphabet backward. Also to finish some of his sentences. Through all this, I was sitting behind, taking the test also. One of the test questions he asked, which I will always remember, was what a tree and a fly had in common. Joe just sat there for a while, thinking about the question the doctor had asked him, and I definitely sat there, thinking about it. I was coming up with a lot of good answers, I thought. Then Joe finally answered the question. The doctor was so impressed when he said, "They are both living things." He looked at him and said, "Normally, people do not get that one right." I know I didn't not get it right.

After about an hour or two of testing, the doctor asked Joe for the three words he was told to remember. The three words were *penny*, *month*, and *flower*. Joe could recall two out of three of the words. The doctor gave him a four-word list a few minutes later, and he struggled to come up with them but eventually recalled three out of four without any problems.

After everything was said and done and all his testing was over at this time, Dr. Reiter and I had a very long talk about everything. He had some concerns and referred us to OHSU (Oregon Health and Sciences University), to a specialist, Dr. Joseph F. Quinn, MD.

Dr. Reiter had the opinion that there was a lot more going on with Joe and that he would be better off seeing someone who could better diagnose him. So Joe at this time was only fifty-six, and I was only fifty-two.

We made the first of many appointments to OHSU, commonly called Pill Hill. OHSU was also a teaching hospital. Dr. Joseph F. Quinn was the clinical trials program director and a care associate professor in the Department of Neurology.

We made it to the appointment on time, maybe a little early, and while sitting in the waiting room, we noticed the place was filling with people that were in their seventies and eighties. I was a little embarrassed as the people there were looking at us quizzically. I kept getting up and down and going to the bathroom to get out of the glares we were receiving, and so that I didn't have to look at them either.

Finally, we were called by the nurse, who at that point looked us up and down, then asked if Mr. Michaud was in the restroom. "What?" Joe and I looked at each other and said, "*No*, we are the Michauds." Joe was the one Dr. Quinn would be seeing. She just looked at us and said, "Please come with me." It could have been funny, but it wasn't.

After the nurse led us to the room, we waited for Dr. Quinn. When he walked in, he looked us both over and said that Joe was going to be the baby of his group. We didn't say a word and just looked at each other.

Dr. Quinn then broke the silence and said that now the fun would begin. He told us that there would be blood tests today, MRIs, CT scans in a week, and more tests to come. But today we'd do some different kinds of testing. He did talk to us for a long time. At the end of all the tests and paperwork we did, he shared with us information, including his impression of Joe, that he was likely to progress to a more clear-cut Alzheimer's disease in about the next three to five years.

We also talked about all the research that they were doing to see what was causing it, why it was coming at all ages, how to prevent it from happening.

Joe told Dr. Quinn that we would be interested in participating in their natural history study, research testing they wanted him to do. He would be up for that. He said he wanted to do everything and anything he could do to help eradicate this disease and why it affected some and not others.

Joe even said that he would donate his brain to science after he died so that they could figure out what was going on in it. I looked at him and said, "We have to talk about this first. We don't even know what your diagnosis is yet or what is wrong with you. Please do not put yourself out there for research till we know everything." All he would say to me was that there was nothing wrong with him;

he would be getting better soon. But if the doctors wanted him to do some more testing to help out on the research, he would be happy to help them out.

Dr. Quinn came back into the room and looked at the both of us. He then said that we would spend a lot of time together to get to know each other. Odd thing for a doctor to say, I thought! But first he would like to bring in Dr. Wild to talk to us. What, another doctor? I was starting to get a little panicky here, because something was going on. Dr. Wild came in and sat down. "Okay," she said, "I need to explain to you about mild cognitive impairment and the onset of Alzheimer's." She was a psychologist in the Department of Neurology.

***"Wait one damn minute.* I don't understand what you are talking about.** I also don't know what the hell these words mean."

That day they told us all about what Joe had: mild cognitive impairment with the onset of Alzheimer's. I had to ask Dr. Quinn and Dr. Wild to slow down and talk in layman's terms.

What was all this? Because I truly didn't have a clue what either one of those diagnosis were. My head was spinning out of control. I wasn't quite sure what I was comprehending.

After they explained to us about what his disease was and what to expect, Dr. Quinn looked at us and said, "We would like to see Joe in six months. This will become our routine."

Dr. Quinn stood up to shake our hands and, as we were leaving, said that he wishes he could have met us under different circumstances.

Dr. Quinn gave Joe a prescription of Aricept and checked on the new appointment as he walked us to the waiting room. Also at each appointment, he said, that they would always test Joe for memory loss to see how he was progressing and do a blood test too. He also said we should contact the Alzheimer's Association. Little did I know that Dr. Quinn would become a regular stop for the next eleven years.

THE LOVE OF MY LIFE

The Day My Life Stopped

Let me tell you one thing about that appointment. When you are sitting in front of two doctors, scared to death, with your mind reeling, not knowing what they are talking about, all you can do is look at them. So we walked out of the doctor's office, with an appointment in six months. We got to car, and I kept looking at Joe. I don't think he quite understood either, so he was quiet all the way home. Now for me, I got mad, then sad, and cried a lot.

I had to do a complete 180 in my life. *What does that mean, what the hell does it mean?* I didn't know what all this meant, but I would learn. All I knew was Joe was my life, my lover, and my friend, also the father of our children.

I was only fifty-two years old, with kids and grandchildren, and a life in front of me.

What was the meaning to all this? What was it going to do to us? What was it going to do to Joe? Was he going to die? I didn't know a thing about this disease called Alzheimer's.

I had to tell the girls at the same time. They were in their early twenties, with their lives and families ahead of them, but I had to tell them, and I also had to tell the rest of the family too and try to keep it together.

I then went online, looked up all about Alzheimer's, reading, and downloading everything I could get my hands on. Then, I went out and got all the books I could get about Alzheimer's: *36 Hours in a Day, The Mayo Clinic for Alzheimer's,* and even *Alzheimer's for Dummies* and *All about Alzheimer's.* I also started to go to a support group, where I also met a lot of wonderful people who were going through the same thing as I was and would be. They were so much older than I was, but they all could help me understand the process.

I read the books from top to bottom and inside out, also marking them up a lot. I did a lot of what they told me to do. It did help, but there was so much more I wanted to learn and needed to know. I also got on all the websites, took caregiver classes, and talked to care people to see what would happen to me, to find out what hell I was going to be going through.

All I knew was that my husband was the most loving, kindest man you would ever want to meet. Even with this disease, he was happy. I believe he was trying to do everything in his power that he could to protect me.

With Joe constantly repeating himself, repeating, repeating. I would get so mad at him that we would get into a fights about it. I knew he didn't understand what he was doing and what was going on, and I was just getting so frustrated with it all, but I also knew I had to learn to work with it. I truly didn't know this was going to get as *bad* as it was. But I did learn real fast the whole effect of this disease.

One day, I asked him what he disliked about himself and this diagnosis. He said that he disliked always repeating himself. Because he didn't know that he was doing it. He also said he didn't know what would happen in the future, as he was the breadwinner of the family, but no longer. Also that he was the father of two girls and a grandfather but didn't know what to do for them.

After that conversation, I stopped talking to him about it. I had to learn to be more flexible with him and with all his questions. Also when he would be repeating something to me, I would act like it was the first time I heard the question. You say something new or say the same thing back to him.

I had to learn to just do my own thing, to help him but not make it hard on him and me, which would help the two of us. I had to learn how to be more compassionate and the ability to care for him without being too judgmental. I also learned that there were enough judgmental people out in public when we would go shopping or do something.

Most people in public were understanding; I know this to be true. But still, some would look at him and see that something was not quite right. One day while shopping at the grocery store, I kept walking back and forth in the aisle. Joe kept following me with the grocery cart. I finally turned to him and said, **"*Just stand here. I am not leaving the aisle.*"** A gentleman that was looking for something in the same aisle said loosely in a derogatory tone, **"I see you have him whipped in place."** In a tone and a deadly look, I informed him that my husband had Alzheimer's. He was very apologetic and slithered away.

After this incident, I realized how difficult going anywhere with Joe would be. In a blink of an eye, Alzheimer's patients can disappear. As time wore on and I wore out, I actually put a bell on his ankle so if he started to leave my side, I would know it immediately. I cannot begin to tell how many times I lost Joe in stores. I can safely say I met many wonderful employees of the various stores who helped search for my Joe.

It is truly hard on family members. Some accept it, and some will not. Many do not understand this disease. It is especially hard on children. Our youngest daughter had a very difficult time with her dad's diagnosis, and she could not handle his repeating himself. She had always known him as her bright, smart, and witty dad.

When she would come over, she would become irritated with Joe because he was no longer the dad she had known. She would constantly correct and many times would yell at him for the things he did and said. By the time she would leave, Joe would always look at me and ask, **"Why does she hate me so much?"** I would tell Joe not to worry about it as I too did not understand it myself.

I found out everyone deals with this horrible disease in different ways. No one knows how a person will react.

Within a few years, I had to get an attorney (the Elder Law Firm) for a new will for us, a power of attorney over Joe, to help start making all the decisions for the two of us and the family. I also got Joe on Social Security Disability and the Veteran's Insurance. All this helped us out a lot. Because Joe's spelling and writing were getting so bad, I needed to know how to protect the both of us.

You go to all your doctor appointment like clockwork every six months, do everything you're told to do. All the testing, all the blood work. But there is one appointment, probably in 2007, that really sticks out in my mind. Boy, does it stick out in my mind

We went to see Dr. Quinn like always for our appointment. Joe was doing okay, if that was what you would call it. Dr. Quinn walked in to do all his testing he always did on Joe. We talked about all the things that was going on at home, then I would walk out to do my paperwork like always. Then after a time, I would get called back into the room with Joe.

Dr. Quinn had all his paperwork on the table. He looked right at Joe and said that he should not be driving anymore. *Oh my lanta*, you would have thought someone had just shot him. He came off that chair then went right off the deep end.

The two of us, Dr. Quinn and I, just looked at each rather than at Joe. Dr. Quinn tried to tell him that he could kill somebody.

Joe didn't care one bit. It was his license, and nobody was going to take it away from him. Dr. Quinn told Joe that it was his duty to notify the DMV. "Go ahead and do it," Joe said, "but I will continue to drive."

After that, I got to listen to Joe complain and complain about it all the way home. When we got home, we talked some more about it. Then I did what the doctor ordered me to do. That next day when Joe was in the bathroom taking a shower, I went through his pockets and got all his keys. Then I went outside and put the club on the pickup steering wheel and locked it up. Yes, living with Joe after all this was not going to be a bowl of cherries, but someone had to do it, for his safety and for the safety of others. Besides that, I'm his wife, so what was he going to do about it.

In time, Joe got to be okay with not driving. Soon, he didn't even think about it at all, and I was now the designated driver; he became the happy passenger.

I did so many things on the spur of the moment that I wish I would have taken more time to think about. I sold the pickup and also our twenty-five-foot comfort trailer, thinking it would help him.

"*Thinking out of sight, out of mind would help us both out.*"
"*Think about it for a long time before you do anything.*"

CHAPTER 4

Becoming a Full-Time Caregiver

Being a full-time caregiver is definitely not a bed of roses or a walk in the park either.

In 2004, Joe was having a hard time comprehending that he no longer had a job to go to. He was never one to sit and wait for something to happen, so along with all the doctor appointments, he buckled down and started looking for another. For months he would send out lots of résumés but didn't get a call, until one day, he received a call from Lincoln Memorial Cemetery; they set up an interview with him. Then in April of 2004 at the interview, amazingly, they offered him a job. They gave him a bunch of paperwork to fill out and also gave him some books to study. There were a couple of younger men who took Joe under their wing and helped him out. I knew something was up when he was having a hard time studying the books they gave him.

He would work so hard trying to comprehend all of it. I remember going to a wedding for my nephew Kerry, on the beach in Seaside, Oregon. Joe would not even come to the reception or join us on the promenade because he kept saying that he needed to study. And that was not like him at all. He always loved to join in with the family and have a good time. I was happy for him getting the new job, so one night we even went out to Men's Wearhouse to get him some new suits to wear at work. I was so hoping this job would work out for him and make him happy again. But I could also see what it was doing to him with all the strain it was putting on him. I just kept saying to him that he was doing a great job and he'd get used to it after a time.

During all this, I started seeing a counselor and started going to a support group at a care facility, which was the one Joe ended up going in. They also gave me a bracelet for Joe to wear in case he got lost. With an ID number on it and a phone number to the Alzheimer's Association in case of an emergency.

Besides Joe seeing the doctor, I also started to see my doctor for high blood pressure. She prescribed me medication for that.

I didn't want to have a stroke, and I definitely didn't want to die. That is the first thing they tell you in all the books you read, that when you are a caregiver to a loved one with Alzheimer's, the caregiver usually dies before the loved one does.

My family and friends with my brother-in-law, Tony, they were all concerned for my health. They would constantly check with me to see how my health was going or if I needed to get out to spend quality time with myself. Which you need to do for yourself. Take up some type of relaxation class, go visit old friends. Just get out of the house sometimes without the loved ones you are caring for.

Joe started his job working part-time but was assured that a full-time position would become available soon. When Memorial Day was approaching in 2004, he was told that he would have to work the three-day weekend. I figured he could use a little break before all those long hours that he would be working, so I told him to take some time off and go up to do some fly-fishing. Mount Hood is one of our national forest with a lot of great lakes to do some fishing in. He would have time to relax, and he also knew quite a few good fishing spots.

I would be able to relax a little too and work in the yard while he was gone. This would work out for the two of us. What a great day it was being in the backyard. I loved working; there for me, it is relaxing. Around 4:00 p.m., I just put a little pizza in the oven for dinner, opened a Corona Light beer for me. Then, I got a call from Joe, saying he was headed to Providence Hospital. He thought his hiatal hernia was acting up. "Okay, I'll meet you there!" I sorta took my time getting there. I had to clean up first.

Because we had been through this before, I knew what the hospital was going to do for him in the emergency room, also how long it would take us there. When I got there and told them who I was, this young man behind the receptionist desk gave me a very odd and funny look. He immediately rushed me off to the room where you know you never want to go into.

I told the young man that they must have made a mistake, because my husband was just having a hiatal hernia attack and to please take me back to see him in the emergency room.

This sweet young male receptionist looked kind of shook up and insisted and said, "Please go into the waiting room and the doctor would be with you shortly." I was starting to get a little nervous that I started rearranging the furniture before the doctor got there.

Finally, a female doctor came in. She said she was from the trauma room with Joe. She also tell me that Joe had come into the ER, went up to the registration desk, started to say his name, and all of a sudden, he went as stiff as a board, flatlined right there in the ER. He fell back so hard that he cracked open the back of his head on the floor.

They called for a code. Joe had died before they got him into the trauma room. They revived him there in the ER with all the other patients looking on, then she told me that the first thing he had asked for was his wife.

All this time I was thinking to myself, *What the **hell**, this can't be happening* and *What is going on? I can't be dealing with two things right now.* But I was right then with Joe being diagnosed with Alzheimer's and tonight a heart attack.

"Okay, okay," I said, **"I'll deal with two things. All I want to do is see my husband."**

The doctor also told me that he would have to have surgery right away, that there was a huge blockage in the lower left part of his heart. They took me to the trauma center to see him. He looked like **hell**. There was blood everywhere by his head, lots of IVs going, but at least he could talk to me. I told him that I loved him lots and lots and kissed him. I would be here through it all. I had to inform the trauma doctors that Joe had been diagnosed with Alzheimer's and of all the medication he was on. I got to walk with him up to surgical area then watch them wheel him away to the operating room.

Then I started to cry. *Oh my god, this man is only fifty-seven, what am I going to do now, and what more are you going to throw at me? What's going to happens if he dies, what will I do then?*

I sat there in the waiting room for a long, long time, thinking about what life would throw at you and hoping that you would recover from it all. I can also tell you that I got so mad I screamed a couple of times with some very, very choice words.

Then I had to get back to the real world. I needed to call the girls and tell them about their dad, then I called all our family and friends to let them know what was going on. It was going to be a long night for all of us.

During the week, Joe was in the hospital. I was doing the bills, which we would take turns doing during our life together.

I came to the reality real fast that Joe had not been paying any bills. He would say he was going into the computer room, do whatever I guess he would do. So when I started to pay the bills, we had a lot of delinquent and past due ones. I believe he lost all his capabilities to figure out the billing. I believe that the computer was getting harder for him too.

Then came his rehabilitation for his heart attack. I called Dr. Quinn right away to see if this disease brought on his heart attack. He said no, it was just something that was going to happen. Joe was in the hospital for over a week and a half. The doctor told me it was a pretty bad blockage that they had to repair. And then Joe got a pretty bad hematoma down by his groin, where they inserted the probe. So they kept him and the bed kinda upside down so all the blood could circulate back down into his body. I knew one thing: Joe was not a happy camper on that move. But after a week and a half in the hospital, everything worked out, and I didn't lose him.

You know, if you continue reading this book (I hope you do), I've never told this to anyone. I don't know if it would have been better for Joe to have passed away when he had his heart attack or what. Because to watch him go through all his pain and suffering, in the end, not even being here really. What kind of life is that for any person to endure?

He got to come home finally after a week and a half in the hospital and was definitely told to take it easy for a while, just start walking, which was okay because Joe and I always liked to walk. Also to check in with all the doctors for all the appointments and medication they had for him. **Yes**, he had lost his job. They talked to me first about why they had to let him go before they told him.

They said he was having a lot of problems remembering things, and it was getting too difficult for him to remember and comprehend a lot of things that he had done or should do.

They appreciated everything he did and enjoyed working with him. But under the circumstance, they had to let him go. After they told him, Joe sat very still. He said thank you to them and walked them to the door. He still didn't talk much about it to this day. Joe never worked another day after that one.

After Joe's heart attack, we started to play Mahjong Titans on the computer. For two reasons, to have something fun to do together and also to keep his mind active. At first Joe would always whip my butt in this game, but the further he progressed in this disease, I could see the stress it was putting on him. So one night I decided that it was time to stop even though he enjoyed it.

It was a good thing we were walkers, but since Joe was diagnosed and after his heart attack, we started walking a lot more around our general area. We made two different routes about four and half miles each, and it would take us approximately an hour to two and a half hours. The one Joe liked the best was from our house up to Glendoveer Golf Course. He could go around the golf course and back to our house. Joe liked this one the best because we got to watch all the golfers play, since he couldn't play any longer; he had lost the capability and his coordination in swinging a golf club. And after his heart attack, it made it so much easier for him to get his exercise.

So with Joe taking his walk sometimes by himself, I always knew the path he would be taking. Which was nice for me. Also the nice thing about it was he had his cell phone with him, one of those old flip-up types. I could glue my name and my phone number if he needed me. So I was kind of sure he was safe, and I knew where he was, hopefully, at all times. You just can't stop their life completely; you have to give them the benefit of the doubt that they can do it.

And that is what I did; I told him if he ever got lost, that would be the end of him walking by himself. And the fear was always there when he would walk out the door. You would always check your watch to make sure of the time and hope for the best. At least I knew he had only the two routes that he would stay on.

But with my average of luck and the way my life had been going, he had to get lost. He went for his walk, and he was in a happy mood, and I knew it would be about two hours or so. I just continued on with my day, till three hours rolled around, and he was not home. Now I was getting a little nervous. Where the hell was he? Not quite sure which route he may have taken, I didn't know which direction to go. I also knew that he did not have a house key either because he had lost two of them already. So I walked out into the cul-de-sac and looked in both directions, hoping that maybe he would come around the corner.

Then I received that dreadful phone call. Joe was lost. He started by saying, *"I don't know where I'm at. I must have taken a wrong turn someplace."* Okay. Okay. I said, *"Tell me what you see around you."* Then he started to describe everything around him. "Okay," I said, *"I think I know approximately where you are. Sit tight and I'll be there."*

The whole time I was driving to find him, I was thinking to myself, Okay, this is the last time you'll be walking by yourself. I'm just so glad you stayed on the same route, because if you didn't, I wouldn't have known where you were. Boy, was he happy to see me. I think it did scare him a little because he was unsure of himself and his surroundings. Thank God for cell phones.

My experience as a caregiver was minimal at best. I was the one who always cared for my Joe. All our friends and family would say Joe spoiled me, so yes, being a caregiver to Joe was something I did not see in our future. And being with Joe 24-7 was not helping me. So to get out, I started taking classes for being a caregiver and caregiving too.

Joe and I gave a lot of interviews on how our lives were before and after the onset of the disease. All the classes helped me out a lot, and boy, what you can learn from it. Also going to a lot of seminars, where you meet a lot of different people who work in the field or have a loved one that has been diagnosed with mild cognitive impairment, or the onset of Alzheimer's, helps too.

I tried so hard to keep our lives as normal as possible and tried to schedule activities almost every day, which was getting harder to do. Trying to think up new and fun things is not as easy as it sounds and with new places to go too.

Joe was always very active; he was a programmer analyst, a computer wiz, and a fly-fisherman. He also made all his own flies and fishing rods. He liked making them out of bamboo. He liked to golf, do geocaching, loved to work in his garden, and we all did a lot of camping and hiking together. He was also a ham radio operator with one of the highest license you could get. Joe and some of his ham friends started a club in 1976, which they called the Hoodview Amateur Radio Club.

He was very involved in the club too. He was the president twice and loved doing it. He taught classes at a local community college and was perfect with Morse code. When you send Morse code, you use a **key**.

It was so sad to see Joe forget how to send code, because he love it so much. He did it in the Navy; also, he could send it faster than a person sending text. He even started to forget the people in the club, which he had known since 1976.

There was always so many hobbies Joe was interested in, and to watch them slowly but surely disappear was so disappointing, and to watch each step crush him and us as his disease progressed.

After Joe was diagnosed, I assumed power of attorney over him, redoing our wills, getting him on Social Security Disability and the VA insurance, and I also started to make all the decisions that we used to make together. Now, I was doing it for the both of us. There would be times when he would get so mad at me and say that I was taking over his life and who did I think I was.

I would try to explain everything again to him and explain why I was doing this. While I was trying to keep my composure, trying to keep my temper, which I can honestly say sometimes just didn't work out too well for either of us.

I remember one time when a friend, Denny, from the club took him up to Larch Mountain for the annual ham radio contest. When you go, it's a camping trip on a local forested mountain, and you would take all your ham radio gear, and if you had a camp trailer, you took that too. You stayed the whole weekend. You would always have to get permission from the National Forest Service to hold the event as it was so large, and it was a *no* camping area, for hikers only. We would always have towers and beams with guide wires all over the place.

There is no electricity or running water too, so you had to bring your generators with you. Denny, our friend, took him. He felt that it would be a great way to take Joe out for a weekend. I did not think it would work out, but Denny had high hopes for all.

Well, during the night, Joe became confused when he had to go to the restroom, so he ended up peeing all over Denny's trailer. That told us that we reached one more step in his decline, one of many, many more to conquer.

Then he started to lose interest in all the hobby and all activity one at a time. We all knew there was more to be concerned about.

Fly-fishing went after his last trip up to Mount Hood. He never went again. One could say it scared him. The ham radios, with the computers, were in there also, including playing all the games he liked.

As a large family, we always try to get together either in the summer for barbecues and always for Christmas and for the birthday party that someone would be throwing. Well, this time it was Cortney's party. She was throwing it for her two boys, Gage and Jones. One's birthday is in May and the other is the first of June. So she decided to throw a big baseball party, with food and cupcakes for all.

THE LOVE OF MY LIFE

At this time, we could see Joe was having problems with all kinds of sports. He was always great doing all of them, but he especially loved volleyball. He would put his heart and soul into this game. His body wasn't as young as he thought it was either. For the next two days, he would complain how sore he was and how out-of-shape he was. Cortney and I knew we'd be keeping an eye on him anyway. Boy, what a great day we had.

We all gathered at the baseball field in broken teams. We also picked up some kids just playing in the park. Have you ever watched the movie *Forrest Gump*, with Tom Hanks? Well, our day was just like that. Like in the movie, when the young girl was yelling at Forrest to run, we'd have to do the same thing for Joe. Someone would hit the ball for him, and then we'd all start yelling, "Run, Joe, run!" We all started laughing so hard, even Joe was laughing so hard. Even when it wasn't his turn, he would just start running. All the kids had such a good time, and this birthday was one we all would cherish and remember.

Then they take a hint, which is what I would always call it. When you can see them go down one more step in this disease. You also know there's no road coming back, and you will have many, many more of these you'd watch them go through.

Joe was always a sweet, kind person with lots of friends and people we didn't even know well, who liked him. He was just that typed of person that when he walked into a room, he drew your attention. He could converse on any subject, and he had a great sense of humor, also a fast comeback with one-liners and jokes.

That was why when we would go out, it made it hard for me to keep track of him. He would hear people laughing, and he would want to go over and join in with them to laugh with them too.

We would always go to the malls to walk around when we first starting dating, also in the first of our marriage years. As a young couple just starting out, you know it is hard to spend money that you do not have. You have so many things that you just truly do need. So going to the mall to walk around was something new to Joe. He liked to do that to see all the people walking around too. Also, he knew that I liked to look at the clothing, so by the time we were done going every other week to the various malls in town, he would pick out the clothing that he liked me to wear.

> *"So for all eight years of caregiving, I now have three closets full of clothes."*
> *"What can I say, I'm a woman. I would always say yes."*

Joe and I loved the Metolius River. It is near Black Butte, in Sister, Oregon. We have been going there since the girls were babies in their walkers. We were camping out of the back of the pickup. You would have to know that there was only dry camping, that there were no restrooms, only outhouses. No electricity either, water came out of a spigot with cold, cold water.

The Metolius is such a fantastic and beautiful place. Joe loved to do all his fly-fishing there; he even taught the girls how to gut all the fish so they could see what the fish were eating on so he could tie up some flies for the next day.

This river comes straight out of the side of a mountain in Oregon; it is in constant flow, constant temperature, and with all the wildlife, you would have to see to believe the beauty. They also have cabins or homes to rent right next to the river. So one year we all descended to rent a big house there, with Joe's whole family. We had brothers, kids, boyfriends, and grandkids and the girls too.

The whole bunch of us in one big house on the river with a deck over the water, you could not ask for more.

We all would go into Sister for lunch to do some window shopping, or for me, just great Christmas shopping. It's one of the best places to go for the whole family. Being there for a week made it for Joe. We would go back to all the old camping spots and to Bridge 99, where he loved to fish by.

After Katrina hit, I was called out for deployment to Arkansas. I was assigned to work with about thirty firemen and police officers. We did the whole west side of the state from the top to bottom, checking on people who lost everything and possibly loved ones too. This one was a very hard job because Katrina wiped out so many lives and property. Then I was sent to Little Rock, Arkansas, to work in the JFO (joint field office) as the receptionist. I enjoyed this job. I got to meet a lot of people coming and going all over the place. We even worked with the National Guard.

Then one day after being deployed for some time back to Sulphur, Louisiana, Joe asked me if I would please stop going out of town. I looked at him and said, **"You don't want me to be deployed anymore?"** He just looked at me and said, **"Yes."** He didn't like being alone anymore. I told him I would see what I could do. I loved helping people.

So for Joe, I stopped putting my name out there to be called for deployment for a few years. After a few years of not being deployed, I received a phone call from my region 10 in Bothell, Washington, the U.S. Department of Homeland Security Office. They were wanting to know why I wasn't on their list to be called, so I told them I would like to take a leave of absence to care for my husband. They said I could not do that; I would have to resign.

That hurt me so much. I liked what I did and because that was a secondary job that I knew I would have gone to after everything was said and done with Joe.

It started to get so hard on Joe, so I got a new job working for a company called Crossmark. I was a merchandiser for the Home Depot stores in Oregon. I would work from 6:00 a.m. until about 1:30 p.m. This was a good time schedule for me because Joe was active enough to take care of himself for the time being.

I knew things were getting bad in October. To add to all the stress, one day, when I was coming home from work, an eighteen-wheeler decided to move into the lane I was in and took me out on the 205 freeway. All she could say was that she did not see me. When her truck blew out my driving window, she picked up the front of my car and tried to pull me in front of her truck.

Then after going down the highway for a while, she threw me and my car off into the guardrail. My saving grace that day was that there was a police officer right behind us who saw it all and could call in for an ambulance. When I got to the hospital, one of my daughter brought Joe to see me. He was not even sure what was going on, and you could see that he had no empathy for me.

He just sat there and looked at me with a very blank look on his face. You could just tell that he did not know where he was or what was going on. I asked one of my daughters to please take him to the waiting room because I hated to see him this way. Thank God I had my daughters still there.

They helped me out a lot with all the housework and helping me with their dad. I had to go to the chiropractor and physical therapist every other day.

Being confined with Joe for almost a year after my accident and not being able to drive taught me patience. Joe truly changed a lot that year. He took some major hits in his disease. And on top of that, I had to look for a new car. Thank God Joe was still driving, but that didn't last long either.

I got a new job with the Portland Water Bureau in emergency management services. It was a part-time job, but it was a job, and I loved working there and being back in the field that I enjoyed. It also helped out that I could work from 6:00 a.m. till 11:00 a.m. So that way, I could get up extra early and make Joe's coffee, get his breakfast set out, and turn the TV on to channel 12 news. They repeated the news for at least four hours, and Joe would not realize they were repeating the same stories over and over again.

So he would just sit there and watch it. By the time I got home, he would have showered and gotten dressed. So that way, we could start our day of doing something fun. I would try to come up with some type of activity every day for Joe to try and keep his mind active. After a while, it did become a problem; you can only do so much for them. Also they may not remember it, but it is a constant repeat for you, and you can only be so happy for so long doing the same things all the time. I tried to suggest a day care for Joe to go to where they dealt with the same disease that he had and in the same stage of the disease also. Joe would have nothing to do with it; he kept saying he wasn't that sick, and he was getting better.

They wouldn't know what they were talking about. There were times that he would get so mad at me and even push me up against a wall and want to know why I was taking over his life. The girls told me one day that if their dad ever hit me, he would automatically be put into a care center, for my safety. I told them that this was my husband and their father and my life with him. And I'd do what I had to do to protect the two of us.

The funny thing is that he did it to me a second time. We were in the hallway, and Joe got upset about something I must have said. He took my shoulders and pushed them right up against the wall and kept his hands there on me. I could see that he was getting madder for some reason. So I had to push him backward and yell at him, **"What the hell are you doing?"** I stormed out of the house and stood on the front porch, staring into the cul-de-sac, with tears rolling down my cheeks and my body shaking. **"I can't do this. This is not Joe at all. What am I going to do?"**

I would have normally ran over to Ms. Yvonne's because she only lived one house away from mine and she had been there through the beginning with all this with Joe. And I knew that she would let me scream and cry all I wanted to. What a godsend she was just being there.

But today I stood there for the time being, just thinking, not even thinking about what he was doing in the house; I really didn't give a damn about him. I was just thinking about me at this point. Then reality set in, and I knew it was not Joe. I also knew that it was the disease taking over him. So like everything else, I had to suck it up and put on a happy face and go back into the house just like nothing ever happened and redirect Joe by asking him if he would like to have a cup of tea or something.

I believe this is the hardest part of this disease for all the caregivers. The people you love just don't understand what they're doing to you or saying. But you do, and you have to move on even if things are happening to you and affecting your family life. You have to always have a smile on your face and also have a nice, calm voice and act like nothing has happened to you. Because the sad thing is they don't remember what they just did to you or said to you. They have lost all sympathy, emotions, and the ability to care and to understand.

I would go to see my counselor about once every two weeks and go get a massage every month because the stress was really doing me in, besides having high blood pressure. I looked like hell a lot of the time, and I believe you age a little at this time too. I do know one thing, my counselor and a lot of my family and friends would always ask me if I were suicidal. Friends would also ask me why I didn't divorce Joe and make it easier on the two of us. First thing, **Hell no, I was not suicidal.**

Why would I do something like that to Joe and the girls? I would not put this on anybody. Also, to get a divorce? Get real. On what grounds would I have to do this for? For one thing, I knew my husband, and he would stick by me till death do us part.

So I would do this for him. Also, that was why we got married, in sickness and in health and for better and worse. I just happened to get the worst of it after forty-two years.

When all this started, I remember Joe was always repeating and repeating himself all the time. I would get so mad at him and then yell at him to stop repeating himself. Then we would get into a big fight about it. I knew he didn't understand what was going on. **Hell, I didn't understand all this myself, but I had to work with him for his sake and mine.**

Joe had to have a colonoscopy. This was definitely hard because of all the medication you had to take prior to the procedure. So we did all that had to be done that day before leaving as you definitely should not leave the house without doing, in case of an emergency.

Finding a restroom by your house becomes a little difficult. The next morning, we headed up to the VA hospital on what they called Pill Hill. They checked him in like they would normally would do for a person who was going to have a day procedure. I stayed with him the whole time, until the nurse said that they were probably going to get him ready to go for his colonoscopy.

"Okay." Then I said, "I'll be off. I'll go down and get some coffee. Call me on my cell if you need anything." So I kissed Joe and said, "I'll be back." Off I went to the cafeteria to get myself a cup of coffee.

I barely sat down when my cell went off. It was the nurse from upstairs with Joe. ***"Mrs. Michaud, your husband seems to be getting agitated for some reason,"*** she said.

"You did not leave him alone, did you? Did you not read his chart?"

She said, "Not all the way through."

"Well, my husband has Alzheimer's, and maybe he just didn't understand why you left him alone. I'll be right up, and maybe you could read his chart before I get there." *I was so pissed.*

When I got back up there, they also told me that he would have to sign his name in the procedure room. **"Are you F@#@ing kidding me?"**

My husband didn't even know how to write his own name, let alone write anything else anymore. So I went in with him into the procedure room. Let me tell you, when this doctor walked into the room, he took one look at me, and you would have thought I had two heads, but if looks could kill . . .

"What are you doing in here?" he said. I tried to explain that my husband could not write his name, and he had trouble speaking. He has had Alzheimer's for the last five years.

The doctor looked at the two of us and still stuck a laptop in front of him with a pen and said, "Please sign your name." Joe looked up at me so confused. "Just scribble your name," I said. He did the best he could, and what a beautiful scribble it was. You know it's funny how a doctor's demeanor can change so quickly. He picked up the laptop from Joe and looked at me and smiled then said, "Could you please sign his name for me?" I did, then I asked him if there was anything else he would need.

"No, thank you," he said, so I said thank you in a very demeaning tone with a look that only a wife or mother could give you. You know, the one that could kill. Then I left the room. Too bad, this doctor could have shown just an ounce of compassion.

In February of 2008, Joe and I went to Cancun, Mexico, where we stayed in a friend's time share. They always went for three weeks, so they graciously invited us to come down to visit. What a great idea to sit by the ocean, have a piña colada or a mai tai, just to relax.

Maybe I should have thought this one through a helluva lot longer.

You do know that you have customs to go through twice with people coming and going in all directions at the Chicago Airport.

When you finally make it into Mexico, you don't speak the language, your husband is trying to visit with everyone, he is laughing and smiling at everyone, and all you want to do is find a bus, get to the condo, and have a large drink.

Thank God we made it to the condo, where we had a fantastic evening sitting outside with a drink in hand, and the view was absolutely gorgeous.

It was getting late, so we all decided to turn in. Boy, was I tired too. I guess Joe was not as tired as I thought because sometime in the middle of the night, Vern was woken up to a knock at the front door.

There stood Joe and a security officer, who asked Vern if this gentleman was a visitor of theirs. The security officer said that Joe got lost. Vern asked Joe what he was doing outside at this time of night, and Joe said he just wanted to go for a walk before bed.

That's what we were told the next morning during breakfast. All in all, we all had a great week there, sightseeing and eating great food. The four of us had a great time together, and I believe Joe truly enjoyed and relaxed. It was a great vacation for the two of us.

Going home was just like arriving. You gotta love the Chicago Airport. Then a funny thing happened. When we finally arrived at our gate to head to Portland, there sat Dr. Quinn. We walked up to him, and I smiled said, "Hello, what a strange place to run into you, Doctor."

He told me that he was in Chicago for a meeting. I looked at him with a smile and said, "Could you please watch Joe for a moment or two?" I never gave Dr. Quinn a chance to say anything as I just turned and walked away. You just have to take any moment to run.

We took our last camping trip in our twenty-five-foot trailer to Seaside, Oregon, at the coast. We would go for three nights to a ham radio convention every year in the past. We would camp with a lot of our ham friends there. We were at the campground, getting ready to pack up and head for home, when this gentleman who was camped next to us in their big motor home walked over to me.

He asked if my husband had Alzheimer's. ***"Why, yes,"*** I said, ***"he does. How can you tell?"***

He looked at me, and he said, "Just by the way he acts."

"Oh," I said, "thank you. I did not know it was that noticeable."

We were off this time by ourselves. Normally we would always go by caravan with all our trailers together, following one another, so we could be safer in numbers. I also knew that I had a friend watching my back on the way home. Also, if I was not driving, I was sleeping, which was not a good sign for me that day. Knowing that Joe was having some difficulty with his driving, remembering his directions, I probably shouldn't have gone to sleep.

Holy Moly, when I woke up, we were right in the middle of a neighborhood block, with cars and kids all around us. Joe was going very slow because he didn't want to hit anything or anyone.

"Where the hell are we?" I said, looking at him. He gave me one of his standard "We're sightseeing."

"Oh hell no," I said. ***"We're lost."*** I had to think fast, told him to just keep driving until I could figure out where the freeway was. "Would you like me to drive for you for the time being, to get us back home?"

"No," he said, "I'm doing a good job here." ***I sold the trailer shortly after the trip.***

I had to start laying out Joe's pills for him because he was having a hard time remembering which one to take for day or night. Then I found out he wasn't even taking them. I also found them in a dresser drawer one day. So now I stood next to him and watched him take them.

There came a time when I would have to start laying out his clothes to wear, help him with his toothbrush, and help him get things ready for his bath.

We would always be looking for his glasses and his hearing aids or something that he would misplace and could not find. He also would said that I moved them, and that would start another argument.

We took our very first cruise up to Alaska in 1998 with three other couples. At that time, I told Joe on our way up there, ***"God help you if I like this," and boy, did I.***

We would take four more trips up to Alaska after that, traveling with our great friends Vern and Diane. Joe loved being in Alaska when he was in the Navy; he was stationed up there in Korea. We did talk about moving up there a long, long time ago. Joe would always tell me that I could stand with all the polar bears and penguins at the supermarket. **Haha.**

If you ever make it up there, you need to go between May and the first of September; that is the only time the cruise lines go up. The scenery and the different ocean life is truly fantastic to see. Get off the ship and all you want to do is walk.

You know, I've learned so much about this disease Alzheimer's, but I need to learn so much more. One thing about the person with Alzheimer's is they take everything so literally.

They make up some very good stories about who knows what. They truly believe what they are talking about or what they did is true. I know of one such incident: Joe loved his merlot. I'd give him a small glass in the evenings to relax him and help him sleep.

Well, one night we were watching TV, a documentary on Alzheimer's, and there Dr. Quinn just happened to be one of the speakers, lucky for us. Lo and behold, he just happened to be talking about a glass of red wine at night. You should have seen Joe's face. You would have thought he just struck gold. Joe also got it in his head that he meant for him to drink an eight-ounce glass of wine or maybe two during the night.

We would go around and around about this one, so I told him that I would pour him wine in a little bigger wineglass; that way, he'd only get one at night.

Then at one of our six-month appointments, I had a long talk with Dr. Quinn. When he made a statement in a speech, he should clarify that he meant only one small wineglass was sufficient, but when he started to talk about what red wine could do for a Alzheimer's patients, Joe took it so literally, that it was okay for him to have more wine than usual because the doctor said so. It was kind of funny to watch Dr. Quinn backpedal and explain to Joe that he didn't mean it that way. One glass of wine would be better than two.

Our last cruise was in September of 2008. We decided to book a nineteen-day cruise through the Panama Canal, figuring since we would be on a cruise ship, Joe couldn't get too far. With Vern and Diane knowing Joe's condition so well, we all would be able to help one another with Joe.

The cruise was from late September through early October. We did adjoining rooms with that common door between us. This helped out immensely, so if Joe got on my nerves too much, all I'd have to do was knock on their door. Alzheimer's patients lose things constantly. There was one day I had my fill. I knocked on the door, opened it, and yelled, **"He's all yours!"** I slammed the door and walked out the other door, where I went to the deck and ordered me a strong drink. It's a wonder I did not turn into an alcoholic. It is common for many caregivers to turn to alcohol for relief.

Joe and I loved to play card games, especially playing gin rummy. I would always kick his butt. The two of us played for hours. Even on camping trips and previous cruises with family and friends. It was getting to a point that he was having a hard time holding all his cards anymore, so we switched to a dice game on that cruise where you had to keep track of your score and add up numbers. Joe could not keep track of his numbers, but he would always win against Vern, Diane, and me. He would laugh and laugh because he thought he was doing such a great job. I always loved to watch him laugh and enjoy himself.

> ***You really don't realize how big a cruise ship can be until you're trying to find somebody that is lost on it.***

Joe would wander off when I went to the bathroom, or he would lose things inside our room. I would go bonkers looking for lost items and a lost Joe. God I love the crew and people in general on a ship; they are remarkably friendly, and they look out for everyone, so after a while, they got to know us and how Joe had Alzheimer's.

Getting off at a port is not a good idea either unless you know where the Alzheimer's patient is. We stopped at one port, and Joe and I went to walk around the city. As we are standing in line, I turned around to tell Joe something, and no Joe. He was gone from my world.

I went from being happy to panic mode in a blink of an eye. I looked for him in ever-increasing circles, but still no luck. I even had some people from the ship and even other ships looking for him. I contacted Vern and Diane. I went back to the ship to see if he had used his key card to get back on, and they said **yes,** he had, but a few minutes later, he had used it again to get off the ship. I had this horrible sinking feeling.

Fortunately, Vern finally found him wandering around, just looking, with no care in the world. Apparently, he went back to the ship to get something then forgot what he went for. With other little mishaps, we did have a great trip and made sure to keep a close eye on him from then on.

I truly do not know what I would have done in such a strange port. (Just happy to have him back with me.)

This was our last cruise ship together. I would miss doing it with Joe. He was always such a great traveling companion to be with.

Our youngest daughter, Morgan, moved up to Ellensburg, Washington, where she was offered a fantastic job in Yakima, Washington, about a forty-five-minute drive from Ellensburg. She eventually met and married her longtime boyfriend and had two children.

This was about a four-hour drive from where we lived in Oregon. When we wanted to go up and visit, I would pack up Joe and the dog, Abby, our Rottweiler at that time. We would usually head up on a Friday morning. It was such a beautiful drive going up Highway 84 through the Columbia River Gorge; we would pass all the waterfalls.

I believe we have approximately one hundred of them too. Sometimes we would stop at Multnomah Falls, one of the big scenic waterfalls in Oregon, and get out, walk around, look at all the water coming off the falls, with all the trout swimming in the river below.

THE LOVE OF MY LIFE

This was the first place Joe took me on our first date. We hiked all the way up to the very top of the falls that day. We would always go up there to the falls and to the fish hatchery with the girls. It was a great family getaway place for us, and the girls loved being by the water, like Joe did. I have a lot of great memories up there.

This was getting harder on me because this man used to be able to talk your leg off. Oh hell, he could talk to you all day long about everything or anything. At this period of the disease, Joe was just starting to have a difficult time putting sentences together, so he basically never said anything unless you would ask him a question or something. Then he would answer you with a yes or no reply.

So I was kind of by myself with the radio, if I could get a good station. Then up by Hood River, I would turn on the CDs.

Four hours is a long time to be without music. I have a lot of CDs that I listen to, but I would always go for Josh Groban. His music would always make me cry or make me smile.

But all I knew was his music would always go deep into my heart and soul. I catch myself pushing rewind all the time. Joe would never say a word. I kinda believe he didn't know what was going on.

He would just smile at me because it was just music to him, and he really enjoyed the scenery and the drive more than anything. The ones I loved the most were **"Your Still You," "To Where You Are," "You Raise Me Up,"** and **"When You Say You Love Me."** I will always listen to them as they make me feel closer to Joe for some reason.

The drive is always so beautiful and absolutely gorgeous going up through Goldendale, Washington, and into all the farmland with the rolling hills. I do love that drive. We were coming into Goldendale, the sun was out, and Joe was so quiet; then all of a sudden he said, "Look over there. On the hill, see the beautiful lake?" What was he looking at?

Oh, I saw what it was—it was a beautiful-shaped cloud that was forming a shadow on the side of the hill. It did look kinda like a lake too, so we had this big discussion about the landscape with everything else we could see on our drive. It was nice to have him sorta talking to me for the time being.

We would sometime stop in Cascade Locks on the way back for some ice cream; they had one of the best twist ice cream cone place there, and Joe truly loved it.

Through the last few years, Joe had changed immensely in his demeanor, his actions, and just being Joe. We had some good days and bad ones, but we kept going. The two of us had a lot of doctors appointments, and I had all my classes and support groups to keep me busy.

But I could see things coming up the pike that were going to change our life for good.

In late August of 2010, we did our last camping trip with Joe. We always loved camping, backpacking, and hiking, just the two of us, and when the girls were young, we started to camp out of the truck with them. Joe always liked being outdoors and by the water.

So Cortney and I decided to do one more camping trip for him, and we all went to Barview Jetty out of Tillamook, Oregon, right in walking distance to the beach. You have to love the Oregon coast for camping; it's beautiful. There are tons of things to do and see, and don't forget the fishing! Joe would love to sit by the campfire and make s'mores with the boys.

We all did a day trip to the Tillamook Cheese Company; they make the best cheeses, and you've got to love all their ice cream too. We all knew that Joe would love to go get him some ice cream, especially chocolate.

The trip did have a few problems, but all in all, it was a good trip. Our grandsons loved walking with him on the beach. He never got lost on this trip because he had three of the best grandsons who loved looking out after their papa for us.

Joe was always a sweet, kind person with lots of friends and with people we didn't even know well who liked him.

He was just that type of person that when he walked into a room, he drew your attention. He could converse on any subject and had a great sense of humor.

That was why when we would go out, it made it hard for me to keep track of him. He would hear people laughing so he would want to go over and join them and laugh with them. He would walk up to strangers and start talking to them as if he was their old friend. He would shake hands with anyone and ask how they'd been and how their job was doing.

That was what happened when our oldest daughter, Cortney, took her father out to do some grocery shopping for me. He walked up to an elderly woman who had smiled at him. Thinking he knew her, he started a long conversation with her.

Who knows what they were talking about? She was very polite and carried on a conversation with him.

Cortney spotted the woman's husband, who could see her talking to someone. He turned around and started to come back down the aisle they were in. She walked up to him quickly and apologized by saying her father had Alzheimer's.

The couple was very polite. They said that they understood. Cortney told him that they had to go because I was waiting for the groceries at home.

The time it really hit home for my little sister, Jolynn, who is seven years younger than I am, was one night when we all went out to dinner for Mexican food; we all loved it. As you know, Joe was diagnosed in 2003, but we still had family gatherings through the years, where Joe was always included.

We are a big family with a lot of kids and grandkids. Jolynn is seven years younger than me, and because of that, she didn't have that much in common with Joe. They were just sister-in-law and brother-in law to each other, but there was always lots of family love between the two of them.

When it came to Joe's disease, Jolynn was one of those that just couldn't see it. She would say to me that he didn't seem that bad, maybe a little forgetful, but not that bad.

If we would go out for dinner, I would have to help him order from the menu; he just couldn't figure it out. My older sister, Linda, could never figure out why I ordered all Joe's food for him. We would always share a menu together and look at the food so I could explain what was on the menu as it was difficult for him to distinguish the different types of food, and reading was becoming more difficult. It was more helpful when the menu showed pictures of the food so I could help him select the food he wanted.

One night, Jolynn got the shock of her life. We were eating at a local Mexican house restaurant on Eighty-Second off Fremont, which we frequented quite often. We would be there sometimes as many as two or three times a week; all four of us loved the food. Everybody in the family loved the food.

While there, we were all sitting at this big table, ad Jolynn was sitting across from Joe. At this point, the disease had progressed to where Joe was having trouble remembering names, even mine. He knew I was his wife, but for the life of him, he couldn't remember my name.

During the dinner, I excused myself and got up to go to the restroom. While I was gone, Joe looked directly at Jolynn and asked her how long she had known me. When I got back to the table, Jolynn had this dumbfounded look on her face.

She looked straight at me and, in a whisper, said that Joe had just asked her how long she had known me.

I just smiled and looked at him. I put my hand in his and, with a laugh, told Joe, "Remember, Jolynn is my baby sister." He smiled and said, "Oh, I know that!" We had a good laugh and enjoyed the rest of our dinner, but when we were leaving, Jolynn kissed me on the cheek then whispered into my ear that she would be calling me soon. Also knew that she would be.

One day early in the morning, Joe came up to me to see what we were going to be doing that day. I truly had no idea what we were going to be doing. All I knew was every time we would do something, something would happen, like when we went to the movies, and when we got out of the movies and went to car, he didn't remember being to the movies.

We had dinner with the family and said our good-byes and headed toward home. As we were heading home, Joe looked at me and wanted to know when we were going to be seeing the kids. He did not remember that we had just had dinner with the kids. I usually just smiled at him and said, *"Oh yeah, you will see them soon."*

Joe always wanted to go on outing and would ask me, "What are we doing today?"

So today I thought long and hard about it and said, "Yes, we are going to go do something very interesting." We were going to go make our funeral plans. We had JW, our grandson of five, with us that day, so I knew we would enjoy it.

But I didn't know if Joe would understand it, but it had to be done one way or the other. I knew all his wishes. Knowing that he was a veteran, I figured it wouldn't be too difficult to do. So off to Mount Scott Funeral Home we all went.

Once we got there, it wasn't really that difficult. I knew that Joe wanted to be cremated, so all we had to do was pick out the program and thank-you cards—we found some that had a lake and a fly-fisherman on it; what a perfect one for Joe—then whatever else came with it. We talked about what my wishes were as well. All I knew was that I wanted to be with Joe. I kept Joe and JW occupied pretty well with showing all the pretty things, all doing some drawings.

But then the fun began when JW and Joe decided to play in some of the new empty coffins, so trying to keep them out of mischief and staying with me made it a good day.

JW would always get into all kinds of debates or disagreements with Joe all the time. I would have to step in and rescue Joe because JW could and would outtalk him and outthink him so fast in a way that would get Joe so mad at him. I would take JW into the living room and try to explain to him that Papa is sick, and he could not comprehend everything anymore. "Just play with him, and he'll be so happy to do that with you."

In July, Jolynn and I took a train trip and went to North Dakota for a family reunion for about a week. It had been so long since I had been back there. I believe I was pregnant with Cortney at that time, and she was in her late thirties. First, can I say, what a trip. It was when North Dakota was flooding.

First we went to the train station like they said too. They then stuck us on a bus to go up to Spokane, Washington. Then we got on a train and headed for Havre, Montana, where we had to rent a car to drive to Crosby, North Dakota. We did the same journey coming back home. I really didn't want to stay away from Joe for too long. So I talked to a great friend who was also a ham radio operator by the name of Pam, who was a CNA (certified nurse assistant). She said that she would be happy to stay with Joe.

I felt much better with Joe knowing the routine of our house. I didn't want him to be out of his element and not sleeping in his own bed.

It already made it kinda easier having Pam staying at our house and sleeping in my bed, because Joe already started sleeping in Cortney's room since 2008. He would talk so much in his sleep, kick and swing his arms and legs, and get up and down all hours of the night.

He told me one night that he did not want to sleep with me anymore. **What can you say, all I know is that it truly hurt my feelings.**

There were times I would go out with friends to have a break, and I would ask them, *"What am I, am I a wife, a widow, a wife in waiting?"* I had no idea what I was. My husband was beginning to not recognize me or know my name.

I guess it kinda worked out for the two of us anyway. One thing I always had in the back of my mind was, and which was my biggest fear, that one night, we would go to bed and he would wake up and not know who I was. It was bad enough that he couldn't even remember my name after being together for over forty-two years.

(That has happened to people with Alzheimer's.)

I would call all the time to check in on him, and what Pam would say was that he was doing great. Never once asking about me or where I was.

So I guess out of sight out of mind.

THE LOVE OF MY LIFE

Our last Cruise Ship trip together, in the Panama Canal 2008

CHAPTER 5

Thank You, God

When Joe got diagnosed with mild cognitive impairment, the onset of Alzheimer's, and after I truly found out what it was and what it did to a person, I was so beyond mad at God and our life together that I ended up having a yelling fit at him. You can probably imagine what I was yelling at him about, but also think what I must have looked like. Thank goodness I wasn't in a car. You have to remember that this was in 2003, and things were starting to go bad since 2001. I was just fifty years old then. Joe was fifty-six at that time. We had our whole lives ahead of us.

We had so many plans that we had made ahead for us and were also working toward them. We were looking forward to being retired together. Joe would always tell me that we were on a fifty-year contract, with renewal options after that. Funny, we only made it to forty-three years.

Everyone kept telling me that I was so strong and that I was doing a great job. I would tell them that you had do what you had to do, that he was my husband and he would be doing the same for me. That was what a strong marriage was.

I also know that God will not give you any more than you can handle. I also know that he is there beside you. But it didn't matter to me at that time, and it seemed as if nobody was going to help me through this. Yes, I know, I did have the girls, but it was so hard on them too, but I also had our family and friends and my core group of girlfriends, with my counselor and my support groups, to share things with, to cry with, but that didn't help; I still felt so alone all the time. Like being in a battle where there was no place to hide and no one to protect you. The one person who was supposed to protect you was gone, and you had to protect him. The feeling of being alone constantly was what got me the most.

Late at night or early in the morning, hell, even just being by myself on the couch was when I would have either a big meltdown or, say, a "why, oh, why me" party or just fall to my knees and cry and pray for Joe.

Sometimes I just truly wanted to beat the holy crap out of something or someone to take the hurt away. I hurt so bad.

I would get so mad at God. I would pray, ***"Can't you stop this? Can't you help him? What did he do to deserve this?"***

I would read the Bible or poems like "Footprints" or others that I like, and I would still ask why.

But one day as I was working on this book, I had a revelation, an epiphany, so to speak.

God is here, he has held me, covered me, walked with me, and I did not have a nervous breakdown when sometimes I thought I was going to. My blood pressure was really high, and I did not strike out because of it. Also I did not get really sick. **Yes.** He kept me strong so that I could go through all this and more. He also has helped me to remember all the love that Joe and I shared together. What I have gone through to be able to write all this down and to remember so much of everything we have shared and also to be able to talk to people who believe they have a loved one who may be going through something like Joe did. You talk to someone whose loved one has been diagnosed with Alzheimer's, and it helps me to know that I can help them with their loved one also.

So thank you, God, for all that you have done for me, but knowing me, I'll probably do a lot more crying and complaining and wishing and begging, so bear with me, and just give me the strength, please, and the love you always have.

> **When God pushes you to the edge, trust Him fully, because only two things can happen. Either He will catch you when you fall, or He will teach you how to fly.**
>
> **—Author unknown**

CHAPTER 6

Celebration of Life Party

In October 2011, I decided to have a party just for Joe, and I called it a **Celebration of Life Party** I did it for all of Joe's family, friends, and coworkers. I did it because I knew that when Joe went into the care facility that it would be the last time a lot of these people would see him until the day of his funeral viewing, or not at all. It was kind of hard on me and the girls knowing this because we knew that date was coming soon.

So the girls and I prepared for the party. Everybody was showing up, bringing food and drinks. Joe did a lot of talking and laughing. Someone was by his side all the time. H e looked as if he was enjoying himself.

There were a lot of pictures being taken because I was going to do a picture book of everyone that attended for Joe to take with him, the party in general. My hope was for all the people, friends, and family who were involved in his life, one way or the other, would just see Joe the way he was. **Happy.**

I did know that everyone had a great time; they kept telling me so. They were happy be able to see Joe. I think they also had the feeling that this would probably be the last time they would ever see him looking so happy to see everyone. They also got to see old friends and coworkers.

After everyone left that night and as I was cleaning up after the party, Joe came to me with a funny look on his face. I asked him what was wrong, and he said that he didn't know a lot of those people, were they friends of ours?

I stood there, looking at him, not believing what he was saying to me. Did he not know what was going on? Or did he just forget that soon? All he knew was that we had a lot of people over to the house today, and they all were laughing and having a good time. I told him that they were there for him, to talk to and have a good time with. He laughed and said that he did have a good time too.

But the sad thing is that he did not know a single person. And with Joe, being the person he is, he would never want to hurt anybody's feelings by asking their names.

The next day, he didn't even remember the party; all he wanted to know was if we were going to see anybody today. I told him, "Of course, who would you like to go see?"

To know that you are going to be putting your husband into a care facility in November, at the age of sixty-four, believe me, that is one thing you will truly never forget.

The sad thing is, you always have to be happy for them, keep smiling while your heart is breaking, doing things behind their back or having to lie to them. You have to do the hardest things to keep you and them safe. When you look into their eyes, you start to see that they are dwindling away from the person that you married and loved so much and needed in your life. To see that they are no longer there. You keep saying to yourself, **"Why him, why me, why us?"**

CHAPTER 7

Joe Moves into a Care Facility

Resident Spotlight on Joe Michaud

Joe was born April 30th to Mary and Joseph Michaud in Portland, Oregon. He has two brothers, Ross and Tony. Growing up Joe and his father had a great passion for ham radios and Joe carried on his passion into adulthood. After graduating from Benson High school he joined the Navy. His ham radio knowledge paid off with the military. He knew Morris code very well and it benefitted him. After getting out of the Navy he met Patricia at an after party. They sat at the same table together and the next Sunday went hiking. The rest is history and have been together since. They were married September 1973 and have two daughters, Courtney and Morgan, who have blessed them with 4 grandchildren. Joe has taken computer classes, worked for the Seventh Day Adventist, a wood company, blue cross and over 30 years for Fred Meyers as a program senior analyst. He also started the Hoodview amateur radio club in 1975, which is still going today. He has many hobbies such as golfing, hiking, camping, ties fly's, makes fly rods, geo cashed and is a member of the stock club with Fred Meyers. Joe is a great guy. He is always in a great mood. We love having him in cottage 1 with us.

THE LOVE OF MY LIFE

PACIFICA SENIOR LIVING PORTLAND — Embrace The World

Ambassador Packages

- **Tuesday, April 8th** — Tulip Festival
- **Tuesday, April 15th** — Build a Bear
- **Tuesday, April 22nd** — Coffee & Pie
- **Tuesday, April 29th** — Breakfast Club

Ongoing Activities

- Monday – Friday: Exercise at 10:00 AM
- Every Sunday: Church Services at 1:00 PM
- Golden Touch Salon: Thursday & Friday, 9:00 AM to 4:00 PM

Birthdays

- 2nd – Christine A.
- 7th – Elsie W.
- 11th – Violet J.
- 16th – Bernice V.
- 17th – Hazel M.
- 17th – Kim E.
- 20th – Dale B.
- 23rd – Connie P.
- 27th – Roy T.
- 30th – Earl B.
- 30th – Joe M.

Weekly Schedule

Sunday
- Morning: Reading, Helping Hands
- Afternoon: Sports Program / DVD, One-on-One Time
- Evening: Devotional / Spiritual, Soothing Hands

Monday
- Morning: Current Events, Range of Motion
- Afternoon: Arts & Crafts, Sense of Scent
- Evening: Snacks & Chats, Puzzle Group

Tuesday
- Morning: Reading, Baking
- Afternoon: Game Club, Music Therapy
- Evening: Movie & Popcorn, Massage Time

Wednesday
- Morning: Current Events, Sensory Stimulation
- Afternoon: Arts & Crafts, Remember When...
- Evening: Snacks & Chats, Listening to Music

Thursday
- Morning: Reading, Helping Hands
- Afternoon: Music Therapy, Game Club
- Evening: Movie & Popcorn, Soothing Hands

Friday
- Morning: Current Events, 1-on-1 / Manicures
- Afternoon: Arts & Crafts, Movie & Popcorn
- Evening: Happy Hour, Massage Time

Saturday
- Morning: Current Events, Game Club
- Afternoon: Old Time Magazines, One-on-One Time
- Evening: Snacks & Chats, Puzzle Group

Special Events

- **Friday, April 4th** at 2:15 P.M. — Cottage 1 Shopping
- **Saturday, April 5th** at 10:00 A.M. — Bingo
- **Monday, April 7th** at 3:00 P.M. — Art's One Man Band
- **Tuesday, April 8th** at 2:30 P.M. — Social-N-Game
- **Wednesday, April 9th** at 2:15 P.M. — Cottage 6 Shopping
- **Friday, April 11th** at 2:15 P.M. — Cottage 3 Shopping
- **Monday, April 14th** at 3:00 P.M. — Patricia Piano
- **Wednesday, April 16th** at 2:15 P.M. — Cottage 3 Shopping
- **Friday, April 18th** at 2:15 P.M. — Cottage 7 Shopping

Happy Birthday

When a patient goes into the care facility, they do what is called a resident spotlight to help the other residents get to know who is coming into the cottage. They also put out a monthly calendar with the activities and any entertainment for the month. They display it very nicely on one of the big walls. It includes pictures and birthdays for the month too.

From the time they are diagnosed with mild cognitive impairment, Alzheimer's, or dementia, you know that somewhere, at some time, you are going to have to put your loved one into a care facility. That opens up a whole new kettle of fish for you by always thinking about it. Looking for a place that is safe and secure for them, which you believe they would be comfortable and happy in, the cost of it and what this would do to you, I believe that this is the hardest thing you could ever possibly do. Even giving birth wasn't that hard. I was in labor for forty-four hours. To know that you are *putting your loved one away for possibly the rest of their life,* **it is like going to hell and back.** Then you start to doubt yourself, feel sorry for yourself, but you know what you have to do.

> ***"Am I being selfish? I can't I do this? What is wrong with me? He can't help it. He's trying so hard."***

But everybody knows his health is going down, he's getting further along in his disease, he is also getting abusive to you, so something has to be done.

You will have family and friends say that it is time, way past time, you should have done it a long time before this.

But then again, you will have family and friends saying that he doesn't seem to be as bad as you think he is. You have to follow your heart and your gut. You have to know what is good for you and, in the end, what is good for him.

"Okay, I finally made the decision." First, have a drink to relax, stop thinking about what you are going to do. Keep telling yourself you're doing the right thing. Call the doctor to see if they have any recommendations for facilities. I then called the Alzheimer's Association and started looking in the phone book.

The next big step was having to tell my daughters what my decision was, that I was thinking about putting their father into a care facility. Knowing that my daughters were married, with kids to care for, jobs, and also that they had lives of their own did not help. I had a lot of empathy for them. I knew they loved their dad. I also knew that they did not want their dad to be put in a care facility. But I had to do what was right for the both of us.

I looked into and called a lot of facilities. I had a lot of questions for them and questions from the family too. Some of the questions I had came from all the books I read previously. I talked to a lot of people that had their loved ones in care facilities also. My daughters also helped choose, because they had a lot of questions too. We ended up picking one that was pretty close to our house.

It was the care facility I had been going to since 2007 for a support group. The support group helped me out a lot.

So I did know a little bit about this facility, but I didn't know exactly what it was like until I had a loved one actually living there.

We finally decided to do it. The one I picked was Pacifica Senior Living Memory Care. My daughter Cortney was not okay with it. She didn't like the idea of her father being in a care facility, but she would stand by me and help me get him in there. I had two good friends, Jackie and Yvonne, who helped us and was always there for the whole family.

Jackie had worked with Joe for years, so this disease was also killing her, seeing him like that. Yvonne was my close neighbor for over twenty-five years, so she saw Joe every single day. When things got bad, I would run to her house just to be able to cry. My youngest daughter, Morgan, didn't like it at all and stayed away.

Sometimes you come up against a family member who is truly having a hard time grasping this disease. Which is a tough one to start with. You will want to help them the best you can, but you may end up having to leave them alone so they can work it out themselves, or sometimes they may never grasp it. I know Morgan would always say she wanted to remember him the way he was. That's all well and good, but you miss so much in the meantime.

Before you can move a person into a care facility, they do what they call a screening of the person you would like to place in their care facility.

This helps them know exactly how far along they are in the disease, also in what cottage they would need to be placed into. Someone from the facility would come out to see them and talk to you and then about what goes on in the cottage.

Joe did not even realize what was going on. They made it so easy and relaxing for the two of us. They were like old friends just dropping by for a visit. When it is time for them to leave, they say all the good-byes to you and your loved one.

She tells you that you will be receiving a phone call to let you know if you've been accepted, for your loved one to be able go into their facility. By the look on her face, I knew that he was approved.

Okay, now I had just jumped one major hurdle; there was going to be a lot more to go.

We picked out a move-in date, and the facility gave us a couple of days prior to move some of his belongings in, clothes, pictures, anything that would make it feel like home to him. I did a lot of shopping to get things that we would need because it was so hard to move his belongings without him getting so confused and upset. Cortney did help by taking her father out for lunch and day trips.

On November 9, 2011, a Wednesday, at 11:30 a.m. we moved him in. I had to lie to him so that I could get him there. Funny, but during all this process, you end up lying to them a lot, and it starts to become easier. I didn't like to lie to Joe. But it is just for their safety or to get them to understand or do something you need them to do. You lie just so that you can move on with your lives for another day.

They first came out into the common area to sit and talk with him for a while. We were all happy and smiling, because Joe liked meeting new people, so everything was going well.

Then they asked him if he would like to come in to have lunch with the rest of the residence. I told him I would be there in a moment; I had to take a phone call first. After that, they took him into what would soon be called his cottage. There was approximately thirteen residences all of them were manning at that time, about in

THE LOVE OF MY LIFE

the same stage as Joe was. I stood there, looking through the window at him, and I started to shake and cry. I knew I had to go home, but I didn't want to. Oh God, this was killing me. I really don't know how I drove myself home or remember it, but when I did get to the house, I cried my heart out.

How could I do this to the man I love so much? He doesn't deserve this. How could I be so cruel? What is he going to do? What am I going to do without him? I kept thinking.

I poured myself a big glass of wine, a water glass size, drank it, and then poured myself another one and kept crying. Now, it was only me and my Rottweiler, Abby, in the house. He was gone, and nobody was here—**nobody.** I crawled into bed, not even finishing my wine; I was too upset to go on. Cortney was going to stop by before she went to work to check in on me. She had with her my grandsons, Gage and JW, but she told them they could not stay while she went to work, which was the usual case. When they came in, they found me in bed. The boys both crawled into bed with me, JW and Gage hugging me and lying beside me.

It felt so good to have someone telling me that they loved me, since it had been over four years since Joe could tell me that he loved me and it would be okay.

I told Cortney to let them stay with me, and that was what they did, lying with me and comforting me on the bed until my Cortney got off work. They didn't want to leave my side; they wanted to be there for me. Cortney and I knew I needed to be alone, and the boys had school the next day. You cannot imagine what those two guys did for me that night. They wouldn't let me lift a finger. They got me all my tissues, water, or anything I needed. Just let me tell you, I love those two with all my heart and soul. They are the ones that saved my life that first night without Joe.

The care facility had a rule that you could not see your loved one for at least a month or two while they were transitioning. Many of the patients would try to break out, have temper tantrums, or anything else you could imagine. I would call the facility day and night during that time just to check in. The facility would tell me that he was doing fine. They also told me he wouldn't put his coat down because he was waiting for me to come get him. He didn't like to sleep in the room because it was not his.

After a month or so, I just couldn't take it anymore. I needed to go see Joe. Cortney picked me up, and we went to DQ (Dairy Queen) before we went to the care facility to get Joe a Blizzard. He loved them, especially a chocolate M&M Blizzard, so we got him one. When we got to his cottage, we looked through the window first to see where he was, then I walked in through the kitchen door, and Cortney walked in through the normal entry to the cottage. He immediately started staring at us with hateful eyes. You could see the anger on his face, and his demeanor was oh so angry as could be.

We walked into the room and sat down at one of the tables. Joe stayed back, just looking at us, and didn't say a word. For what seemed like an eternity, Cortney and I just sat there, but finally, Joe came over to us.

I asked him if he would like the Blizzard I brought for him, but he yelled back at me, which he never did before.

"No, I want to go home, now!"

Finally, I calmed him down enough to get him to sit with us. He was still so mad and was starting to cry. Cortney was starting to cry too, but I knew I had to be strong and not cry. He kept saying to me *"What is going on? Why did you leave me here? I want to go home."*

He wouldn't even let me hold his hand or touch him, as the Blizzards were melting. Nobody wanted to eat them.

I told him, *"Joe, you've got to trust me. You do trust me, right? You know I wouldn't do this to hurt you. I love you way too much for that. I'm doing this for your safety and mine. Joe, I will be here every day if that's what you want. I will take you out on outings occasions too. But you have to stay here now and make it your home."*

We talked some more about it, and he finally came to the conclusion that it was probably best for him to be in this place.

I promised to come see him every day, and that's just what I did.

The care facility was split up into eight cottages, and the cottage he was in, cottage 1, was the elite cottage, or was better known as the ambassador cottage.

This was where you would stay if you were still mobile, could dress by yourself, and shower and feed yourself. This cottage was allowed to go on outings. They would do things like bowling, fishing, and golfing.

We all knew that Joe loved those two things. They would also take trips to the beach to have lunch. They went to the tulip festival. Once they went to a place where they could make pottery. Joe loved that and would show off the things he made. They went to an aviation museum and to other museums.

Joe and all the guys would love touching the things and talking about them. They had great fun on these trips. Outings were scheduled throughout the month. They would also help out Tim, the handyman of the facility, with painting project for the bazaars they had once a year or would work in the courtyard, which had a path to walk around on, benches to sit in and watch all the birds. Yes, it was always locked for safety reasons.

They were also taken to another facility to help the residents there. Joe made a lot of new friends in his cottage. I would walk in, and there they would be, sitting at one of the dining tables before lunch or even after eating, having coffee. They would be talking or trying to talk. Even when their speech would get all mixed up, they continued on and enjoyed themselves. They talked about being in the service or just reminisce about what their lives were like and where they worked.

Some of them were further advanced than Joe and could not communicate at all. But they would still sit there and smile and laugh, just having a good time listening.

I would always come in and sit next to Joe, or they'd have a chair waiting for me. They always knew that I would be there before lunch, because I always had lunch with Joe. I enjoyed sitting there, listening and laughing with them and making up really dumb jokes to make them laugh or singing songs to the radio. Just let me say, I have a very, very bad voice for singing.

They also had special events that would happen either during the day or on weekends. All kinds of events, like sing-along, dancing, barbecues, something for everyone. Cortney, Jackie, and I would go to a lot of these. We would always end up dancing with all the gentleman, and could they boogie down to the old classic ones, with some good slow ones in there too. Joe made so many new friends, especially one whose name was John.

The two were inseparable; they even had to move the two of them into a twin room together so they could visit when they wanted to. The two of them were as different as night and day. John had no family to speak of, so we became his family. His job was as a flamingo dancer, and at his age, he was so limber. He would love to dance with me when the music was on. We always liked to be nude a lot, especially during the summertime.

Joe was a programmer analyst, married man with kids and grandkids. They truly enjoyed each other's company and watched out for each other. John had been there six months before Joe and could still speak quite well. They would help each other out if something came up or if one of them didn't understand something.

In July, Joe went into the great room, where they had a lot of chairs and recliners and a TV. He started taking off his clothes. He was trying to go to the restroom, but he didn't know where it was. We all started talking about maybe putting him in an adult onesie. It would help him by not making it so easy to take off his clothes. A lot of the residents wore them; it makes it so much easier for the caregivers.

I would always go pick up Joe and John and take them on day trips up to the Columbia River Gorge to look at all the waterfalls or to the mall to walk around and do some window shopping. John was good at picking out things for me to buy.

I would take Joe out for day trips to do something fun or pick up him on Sunday nights for dinner at Cortney's house.

One night after dinner, we had a big bonfire in Cortney's backyard. We always made s'mores, which Joe loved. We would add extra chocolate on his too. We would have all the family over so they could see Joe; he loved that. Even though he didn't talk much, he loved to listen to everybody laughing and joking with him.

One night when Joe was over at the house, we opened a bottle of merlot for him; this was his favorite wine. We were always allowed to drink when he was out of the facility and with us. He was happy to get his glass and just sit there, visiting. No one paid attention to him drinking his wine. Whenever it looked empty or getting close to being empty, someone would fill it up. He was drinking it like water. We guessed, between all three of us, Cortney, Buddy and myself, no one was checking the quantity he truly was drinking.

That night he had quite a lot of wine because nobody knew that the other person was refilling his glass. When Cortney and I took him back to the facility, and it took the two of us, we realized just how drunk he was. We had to walk him to his room and drop him in his bed. We covered him up and kissed him good-night. When we were leaving, we told the caregiver that was on duty that night that he would probably not be moving at all tonight but to please keep an eye on him. From that night on, there was only one person designated to refill Joe's glass.

Memor Garden
2011

The walk for Alzheimer's,
with his daughter Cortney.
2012

All of Joe's friends he made, in the Elite Cottage 1 (2011)

CHAPTER 8

Downward Spiral, April 2013

You know how your Friday is going quite well. You've been to see your husband. He's had a great lunch, and he is in such a good mood for being April 2013. I know that he will be going outside for a long walk later, which he always enjoyed doing.

All the cottages have their own courtyards in the back so they can walk around or just sit to get some fresh air. There are benches there and bird feeders and a concrete path. But then it all comes crashing down on you. You receive a phone call around dinnertime. They tell you that they have to do an incident report for Pacifica Senior Living on Joe. "Why do you need to do an incident report on him?" I asked. I guess when he was out walking around on the path to get his exercise, he tripped and fell.

With Alzheimer's, they don't have the comprehension to think about using their hands to block their fall; they forget to put their arms out to protect themselves. He fell hard on his face and had a hematoma over his right eyes. I talked to the nurse who was on duty. They always have to call you when something like this happens, then they fill out their incident report.

I asked her, "How bad is it? Do you think he should go to the hospital?"

"No! It doesn't look that bad," she said. I told her, "Okay, then I'll trust your advice, but I'll be there soon."

Sorry to say, I did not particularly like this nurse on duty, and I did not believe a word she said. I decided that I'd better get there sooner rather than later to check him out for myself. I was happy I did.

I walked into his cottage, and there he was, sitting at the dining room table, waiting for his dinner with the rest of the residence.

"Oh my god!" I screamed. They had him sitting at the dinner table with a massive hematoma the size of a baseball over his right eye, dripping blood down his face.

I can I honestly say I lost it. "What the hell is going on in here?"

I started to scream at the two young caregivers. ***"Do you really think he is going to eat dinner looking like that? He needs to be in bed with his feet up and elevated!"***

I got some wet washcloth and applied it to his forehead. I sat with him, changing his wet washcloth out and just keeping him company. I called Cortney, who came right over to help me out and to see how her dad looked. I also told the caregivers that he would be having his dinner in his room tonight, that is, if he wanted to eat. Then I wanted to know, ***"Where is that damn nurse at?"***

His face was not going to be a pretty sight for at least a couple of weeks. I kept putting wet washcloth on the bump. I also gave him some aspirin because I knew they'd have to get a doctor's request for something like this, and I wasn't in the mood to wait. By the time the two of us left, the swelling was down a lot. He was going to have a big shiner with some scrapes and bruising. I never did see or talk to that nurse that night.

But by God, I did have a talk with Dana, the executive director of the facility.

Having Alzheimer's, they cannot describe their pain or even know what it is, and it is sad we don't know if they're hurting or in a lot of pain. All we can do for them is go by the way they look or if they are grimacing.

He was getting back into his old routine after his fall with help from John. He was even back walking outside like always, watching all the birds with his friend John. Everything was going great in my book, till I got a call sometime in early May.

They found Joe sitting down in the courtyard, having a good time eating the rocks. They checked him out to see if any of his teeth got broken or if he still had any in his mouth. They could not say if he swallowed any of them, but all we knew was if he did, he would hopefully pass them. I love and hate those incident reports. You know they have to do them for the protection of the residents and themselves.

So you will always know what is going on when you are not there, but all it was telling me was he took another hit in this disease. I do feel sorry for the caregivers and the staff; with the disease, the residents do so many off-the-wall things. They keep everybody on their toes all day long. After this, Joe was no longer allowed to go outside by himself anymore. He was not happy about this at all. He would start to bang on the back door because he couldn't get it open. Thank God they always kept it locked for everyone's protection after that.

After the incident, this was when Joe started to get combative. He never had a mean bone in his body, but something in him was changing. He was even getting combative with some of the residents. He would try to hit you or chase you around the cottage.

On one of their outings, they went to a golf course. Joe loved to golf. We had golfed for many years together. But he took out a golf club and tried to hit one of the caregivers with it. They finally got it away from him. Someone took him back to the bus for the rest of the day. You've got to remember, Joe was a very strong man, even with Alzheimer's. He was no longer allowed to go on an outing after that incident.

In all the books that I read, they said that this disease usually would turn a sweet person into a combative one or a combative person into a sweet one. Joe was now becoming very combative, and he could change on the drop of a dime. I would always joke with Dr. Quinn that if I ever developed Alzheimer's, I would be a bitch on wheels before they even begin to think about putting me into a care facility.

At that time, he was also starting to lose his ability to speak more and more. I do feel that it would be such a hard thing for anyone to go through it, including Joe, who was such an outgoing person.

I know it was definitely hard on me too because he wasn't talking to me at all, and to lose the sound of your husband's voice is something you can't get back or remember. It's hard because all you want to hear is that he loves you a lot, but you get nothing. The knowledge that they're losing the ability to communicate is devastating enough.

They have so many stages with this Alzheimer's disease that they go through, and everyone is so different in so many ways too, but they are so alike also.

There are the spitters, the gropers, the throwers, the hoarders, the remodelers, the punchers, and the cursing Joe was now at the phase of not talking, having trouble walking, and becoming combative. (What fun.)

In June of 2013, I went to see Joe, as I always did, and he was sitting in the great room, watching TV. I asked him if he wanted to go out and have lunch. He said, in no uncertain terms, **"No!"** That was the one word he could always say. All of a sudden, Joe fell over, unconscious. My heart stopped. I thought he had just died on me. I screamed for caregivers. They came running and called the nurse at the same time. They also called 911. While we waited for the ambulance, we did sternum rubs, and when the EMTs (emergency medical technician) got there, we finally got him back, but just barely.

They started to ask him some questions like, "Do you know your name?" or "What day is this?" and "Do you know where you're at?" I looked at the nurse and asked her if they knew where they were at. This was a memory care center, so what the hell were they doing? They told me that they would be taking him to Providence Medical Center. "Okay, I'll meet you there."

When we got to the hospital, they had to start doing lots of tests. The nurses wanted to do an EKG (electrocardiogram) on him and some blood work too. That was so much fun with two nurses, Cortney, and I holding him down to draw blood. Then came the IV (intravenous therapy). He was slightly dehydrated; they don't drink enough water like they should do.

They could not keep the IVs in for long because he fought with all the tubing. They ended up keeping him overnight, so I stayed with him in his hospital room.

That was not a fun night for me. No sleep at all.

He was in an unfamiliar place and so out of his element and just didn't like being there. He constantly fought, trying to get his hospital gown off, and kept trying to get out of his bed, with the buzzer going off all the time, which didn't help either.

This was also very stressful on me because my two loving daughters, Cortney and Morgan, hadn't talked to each other at all since before we put their father into the care center back in 2011. That put a big strain on me because my family now was split in two. They both came up to the hospital, walked into the room and divided. They wouldn't look at each other or talk to each other. All I knew was they were there to support their father and me.

The tension in the room was so bad you could have cut it with a knife. Even the nurses and friends could felt it. It was so hard on me. I wanted to be there for my husband, and you also want to be there for your children, but which one? All you can do is love them equally. Before he could check out of the hospital, they had a physical therapist come up to see him. They wanted to see if he could use a cane, a walker, or a wheelchair.

Joe could not comprehend how to use either one of those. This told us a lot; it told me he took another big hit, and what to look for. We got to take him back to the care center the next day, but all they could tell us was it might have been brought on by the disease.

We went to the hospital three more times that summer, each time to a different hospital. Each time the EMTs were called in, I would tell them that he could get very combative, so they should be prepared. I'll always remember this one time, I told the head EMT person, "Joe gets combative. He might take a swing at you."

He looked right at me and said they knew what they were doing. Okay. I was standing in the emergency ambulance doorway at the hospital when they unloaded Joe. The gentleman got out and looked right at me with a huge bright-red cheek. **"You weren't kidding about that," he said.**

I can remember another time we had to go to the ER, and this sweet male nurse was assigned to Joe. He wanted to get a urine sample to make sure that Joe did not contract a UTI (urinary tract infection). I told him, "Well, you better bring in a lot of men." He gave me a funny look and said he thinks he could probably handle it by himself. I told him, "There will be no chance in hell you'd be able to handle it by yourself," and walked out of the room.

Thank God he listened to me, and you could see on his face afterward that I was right. After that, they always would bring two to three nurses in at a time. It was the same each time because he would get so far out of his element.

You could see a big change in Joe that year and the different phases he was going through. He was so out of character from his usual self. Yes, I knew it was the disease, but what else was going to happen with him? All this was so new to me, and the books don't tell you a damn thing about how to react or what to look for. It is all a guessing game. What's coming next? How well are you and your family going to survive through this? Those are the big questions.

September 2013, Joe pushed one of the female residents down. She got in his face and was asking him where her mother was. Because he could not talk, he was trying to get away from her, but she kept moving in front of him. So finally he had had enough and pushed her down to get away from her. He pushed her so hard he fell himself. The daughter of the woman resident was none too happy about this and wanted Joe moved to a different cottage.

They moved Joe to cottage 4. They always try to keep them in the same general area of where their rooms were in the old cottages. Therefore, they don't get so confused and walk into a new residence room.

They also had to move his friend John to cottage 4 because he kept looking for Joe and calling him; he was missing him and was getting agitated without him. Things went well for a while. They were giving Joe a PRM to keep his temper in check.

They would mix it with chocolate so he just thought he was getting a treat. We all know how much Joe loves his chocolate. He was now in Depends also because he could no longer remember to use the restroom or where it was anymore. We could see that his walking was starting to get really unstable and very wobbly; everyone was getting concerned, including me. I didn't want him to fall and hurt himself or someone else. So just before Thanksgiving, Pacifica put in a call into Gentiva for Joe to start getting into hospice.

I had already met a few of the people with Gentiva before, just by being there all the time with Joe and also two of their pastors. I knew of them, and they knew of Joe too. They also believed it was time for him to be receiving hospice. I remember this day so vividly, the day we had our initial interview.

A very sweet woman by the name of Janice came to meet with Joe and me to do all the paperwork for Gentiva. We were sitting in the common area of the cottage. I was sitting next to Joe in a rocking chair, while Janice sat facing us. She was telling us everything we needed to know about the care that Gentiva would be doing and giving us. I told her about Joe and myself and what we had been going through since 2001.

Joe was just sitting there, playing with my hand and arm like always. All of a sudden, he started to bend my wrist to the point where I believe he was going to try to break it. I looked into his eyes, and I could see he was beginning to get that agitated look.

I told Janice that I would be right back in a minute. I pulled my arm free and jumped out of the chair to get to the med room to have the caregiver give him a PRM (as needed for pain), which took me approximately two minutes.

By the time I got back, Joe had already knocked all her paperwork and books out of her lap. I yelled at Joe. He looked up at me. I told Janice to move back slowly. I knew he wouldn't hurt her, but I didn't want to take any chances. She looked kind of shaken up anyway. They brought him his PRM and said, "Here you go, Joe, chocolate," but instead he yelled, **"No!"** Joe didn't even notice that we had gotten up and left the area.

As we walked to another part of the building so we could finish our business, I was apologizing to Janice for Joe's outbreak. She told me not to worry about a thing, that he was already approved for hospice. I looked kind of shocked but said "Thank goodness" to her. We continued to talk about all the ins and outs and everything that hospice does for their clients and for the family.

Let me say this, *thank you so much to Gentiva for all they did.*

They have everyone and everything that any one person could ever ask for to care for your loved ones.

On December, Joe was having a real bad day. He could not or would not get out of his bed. He was pale, and he kept talking to some imaginary person in the corner of his room. The caregivers said they would put a call to hospice to see what they could do.

Hospice then started him on what they called comfort mess. We all hoped that it would help, and it took some time, but he finally started to calm down and fall asleep.

The day before Christmas, I received a call from the care facility. Joe had fallen down four times that day and was throwing up. He was lying on his back in his bathroom, and they were trying to roll him to his side so he wouldn't choke and aspirate. Joe was a big man, so they had to go get a big man to help them out. Thank God they had one that worked there. It took the two of them to do it.

Hospice started ordering him wheelchairs; he was becoming unstable on his feet and falling down all the time. Joe was a big and strong person. He broke three of them in four months. He would roll it backward, forward with his feet and then fall out. Then he would move it with the brakes on or wrap his legs around the leg rest and fall out. Dave, one of the nurses with Gentiva, and I came up with an idea to make a footstool that would fit partially inside of the wheelchair and wide enough on the outside of the chair so he could rest his legs in it. That way, he could not wrap his legs around the legs of the chair anymore.

There is nothing like this out there on the market; we looked. So I decided to build it myself. I am my father's daughter, so we could build anything and everything, and Joe could do the same. I wasn't afraid to try it either. I just had to draw it out and measure it. Dave and I talked about it and came up with a plan.

I went to Home Depot and started looking for what would work out for me to build the footstool. One of the sale associates by the name of Nick approached me. He came up and asked if he could help me find something.

I explained to him what I was trying to make. I showed him all my drawings and the measurements of the stool and explained how big it needed to be. I had it all right down to how it should look when finished.

I explained to him what it was going to be used for, about Joe and his Alzheimer's and the stage he was at right now. Nick asked me if he could keep all my papers with the measurements and diagram; he would get all the supplies together and give me a call when they were ready for pickup.

A week went by, and finally Nick called, asking if I could come in to the store. I told him that I'd be there in about an hour. Nick met me at the customer service desk.

With him was the store manager, also a couple of other associates from the store, one of whom was named Mark. This made me a little nervous because all I was doing was coming in to pick up the parts to make the footstool.

But instead, they pulled out a finished footstool from under the counter. It was beautiful, painted, and they padded it too. What could I say. I also couldn't help myself; I started to cry and gave hugs all around.

Apparently, Mark had a family member who also had Alzheimer's; he just wanted to help out. What he did was perfect; it was beautiful. All I can say to Home Depot is a big thank you for your loving help. I couldn't wait to get it back to the care facility and show it off.

At first, the footstool worked real well for him. He was doing pretty good with it, but after a while, he kept slipping down in his seat, arching his back. That way, he could get his legs to move around it easier, and it would move a little at a time. We used Velcro to attach it to the floor, and that worked for a while too, but he kept working at it, always hurting his legs by trying to move it around. Hospice started to look for a new wheelchair for him also.

The third wheelchair we received was a reclining chair, with a high back so he could rest his head and support his back so much better. Also, Joe's feet could no longer touch the floor this way. With Alzheimer's, sometimes they want to get out of the chair one way or another, even if they don't know why they're doing it.

We also started to get Joe on some kind of routine; they are always in some kind of a routine, but with Joe being confined to his wheelchair, it didn't help. The caregivers would get him up in the morning, get him dressed, and he then would go have breakfast. After a couple of hours, they would put him back in his bed to rest. Then before lunch, they would get him up again to eat and watch some TV. After that, they would give him a bath and let him rest again. The hospice people would always do that for him. All this was to help him not get so sore from sitting in the chair, leaning back all the time, and also to help him stretch out a bit.

After a time in cottage 4, they decided that Joe should be moved to cottage 5. One thing about this cottage was they were all male caregivers with all male residents in it. They could do all the lifting and moving of Joe much easier, because there were all women caregivers in cottage 4, who were not as strong as the men were in 5.

About six months after we got married, Joe decided to grow a beard. The older he got, his beard became a beautiful shade of gray. He would always keep it a very tight-trimmed beard. He always looked fantastic in it, and it went with his beautiful blue eyes. One day, he cut it off without saying anything, which blew me away. **"What are you thinking?" I said.** This wasn't the man I married, so he started to grow a goatee.

Well, with his disease, I tried to keep it trimmed so it looked good. What did I know. When he got moved to cottage 5, the head caregiver in the cottage was a gentleman by the name of Memo. He looked at me that first day and asked, "Are you the one who is trimming his goatee?"

"Yes," I said.

"Please do not touch his goatee anymore. I'll be happy to do it for you."

I didn't think it looked that bad, but I was happy to oblige.

After they moved Joe to cottage 5, John, his friend who moved with him to cottage 4 as they had become such great friends, was having a tough time. John did not progress as fast as Joe did. Alzheimer's works in mysterious ways. He got so unstable and confused all the time after Joe moved out of cottage 4. One night he fell looking for

Joe, and he broke his hip. They had to hospitalize him for two weeks, then they had a caregiver stay with him in the facility so he would stay in his wheelchair, but he kept trying to get out. This became so hard on him. He was also getting so weak that after a time, he just stopped trying to get up. After that, he stopped eating and drinking anything.

One of the many problems with Alzheimer's is that patients forget how to chew or swallow. Many of them die because of this, and John was now in that phase.

He could no longer swallow. We even tried giving him water by a syringe, but that didn't help.

On May 7, 2014, John passed away. Mary, the wife of another resident, and I sat there with him as he passed. We had become John's family as he had no one but us to speak of. It was no use telling Joe what happened. He wouldn't have remembered him anyway. Alzheimer's takes away any empathy you may have in cases like this.

John will be missed. He is up in heaven with his mother, whom he loved so much, and all his friends. God bless you, John. You will be missed.

In April, Cortney called me to say that she would like to do a tattoo of one of her dad's fishing flies that he always made to go fishing with. I said, "What a great idea to have a remembrance of your dad like that." We now have matching tattoos in memory of him.

As of May 2013, Joe was no longer smiling at me when I walked into the cottage to visit him. I think he truly could not remember who I was anymore. But my saving grace was that sometimes, he still puckered up to give me a kiss. I kept wishing and hoping that there was something of a glimmer of me in his brain.

To lose their voice and not remember the sound of it, to lose every thought of you and your family is a hard one to take. Their eyes get fixated like tunnel vision; you don't even know if they're looking at you or what they are thinking. But all you know is that you want to be there by their side.

The sad thing about this disease is a lot of people cannot cope with it. Even though it's a family member or a loved one who has this disease and is suffering from it, they are the ones who get put on the back burner.

I have seen two residents, one from California and one from Alaska, being brought to the care facility and dropped off, with no one coming back to visit them or calling them at any given time. To me, that is the cruelest thing you could ever possibly do to a person that you were supposed to love. They are so confused and out of their element. No wonder they get so angry and combative. This will make them take a major hit in this disease. One of the residents who was dropped off became so angry and out of sorts he went into another resident's room during the middle of the night and beat the holy crap out of this resident before the caregiver could arrive. Both residents were taken to the hospital.

One morning, Joe started having hallucinations. It was scary, because he was talking to things and people that were not there. His arms were flailing all over the place, and all I could do was sit with him. I couldn't even hold his hard. After a time, he calmed down and just snapped out of it, and it was good to see him look so peaceful.

It is so sad to see all the residents and what the disease does to them. They might have been doctors or lawyers, programmers like Joe, professional people of all walks of life, but they are no longer with us. And what they go through with this disease is something you would never think they would turn into. Every day they slip a little further into the disease.

I had requested with Gentiva that Joe receive a bath three to four times a week because it would help him to relax his muscles and make him feel a lot better. One of the caretakers from Gentiva was the one who was doing all the bathing, and he was so good with him.

Joe had a great day on June 11. It was the day the care facility had an activity Joe could participate in. This one was for Father's Day Seafood Bail with the Sunset Traffic Jam Jazz band in to entertain us. We all went to it; there was Cortney, Jackie, myself, of course, and we even got Ross to go. Ross was one of those people in his stage of Alzheimer's that didn't like to travel very far from his cottage. But we all talked him into it anyway. They sat next to each other, Ross knowing Joe, but we all knew that Joe did not recognize Ross at all.

The two of them seemed to be having a great time. Jackie mentioned that Joe would sometimes clap his hands together to the beat of the music and then smile. Because with him not having motion all the time, it was great to see him react. It would bring tears to my eyes, but it was so good to see, but it didn't last for very long, and then it was gone.

What their brains react to and what they don't react to is so hard to understand. The band entertained us for forty-five minutes. They had to prepare for the second show. With so many cottages, they had to break it up into two parts.

As we were all leaving, Cortney was wheeling Joe back to his cottage, while I was walking with Ross. All of a sudden, Joe spotted Ross, and his eyes got real big, and he smiled (that was such a great moment to see). But then we went back to reality, and Joe went back to where he was. Father's Day came and went, and we were back into same routine as always. With me trying to feed Joe his lunch and trying to keep my spirits up as he declined even more. He would look so tired to me, so I would ask Memo if he was sleeping okay, and he would always say yes. But I knew that Joe had always been a good sleeper. I said, "Let's just put him back to bed to rest then." I kissed him good-bye and cried all the way home.

Later that afternoon, Cortney and Buddy went up to see their dad. They said when they got there, he was still in bed. Joe looked directly at the two of them and said, "Hi, Bud," as plain as day, which definitely made their day.

One day when I went to see Joe, he was in great mood. What threw me was, for the first time in a long time, Joe turned his head and looked straight at me. Then he tried to sit up in his wheelchair to give me a kiss. Which he had not done for almost a year. You have to know, with this disease, Joe had developed tunnel vision. It's like looking through a pipe all the time. So to have Joe do something like this, **you have no idea how that made me feel, for that brief moment, to have the one person whom you love so much, to have him back like that.**

I was sitting with Joe, just holding hands, watching a soccer game on TV. I saw one of the other residents walk into Joe's room.

I knew that he was prone to taking things off the wall, rearranging furniture. Often in doing so, he would break things. I got up and walked into the room behind him to tell him, "This is not your room but Joe's." You have to do a lot of repeating to the residents, because some of them like to wander.

He was just standing by the window, and I thought maybe he was just there to look out into the courtyard, to see the birds and the squirrels running around.

To my surprise, he wasn't just looking out the window; he was peeing into the heater vent that was below the window. I called for one of the caregivers to help get him out of the room and to help clean up the mess.

They called the maintenance people to come and do a thorough cleaning job on the unit. (Just another day in a care facility.)

Havest Ball in Set 2013
Joe is 66

Our last Christmas together, with family 2013. Swad Jackie

THE LOVE OF MY LIFE

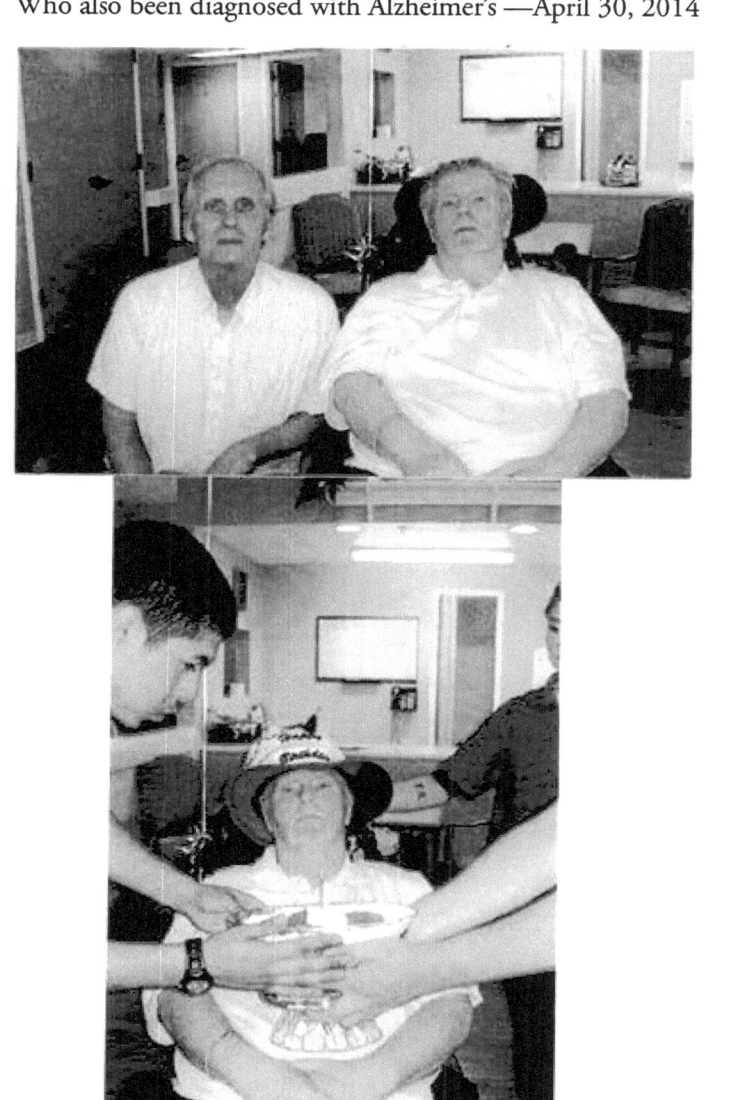

Joe on his birthday, he turns 67. Here with his brother Ross. Who also been diagnosed with Alzheimer's —April 30, 2014

CHAPTER 9

Ross's Diagnosis

Resident Spotlight on
Ross Michaud

Ross was born in Portland, Oregon, on September 11th to his parents Joe and Mary. He has two brothers, Joe and Tony. They had a lot of cats growing up, that explains why they have such feelings for our house cat Sweetie Pie. Ross attended high school at Benson High School. His favorite class was auto shop. After high school he joined the United States Air Force and was stationed in Florida. Ross loves to walk, he does that most of the day, but he likes any physical activity like riding bikes or hiking. He also likes to travel; he has made many trips to Vegas but also loves places here in Oregon such as Multnomah Falls and the Beach. Besides be active outside he enjoys woodworking and auto work. He has two daughters Erika and Amy. We enjoy having him here in Cottage 1.

You know, with all the trials and tribulations we all had been going through with Joe, who would ever have thought that there would be a brother too coming up the pike to be in line with Joe, to get this horrible disease also. Ross is Joe's middle brother; he is six years younger and is fifty-seven. Then there is Tony, who is nine years younger and is fifty-four.

Ross lost his job in 2011. That summer, he was beginning to act strange, which we all took notice of when we were together as a family. Having watched Joe, we could see a similarity in Ross. Boy, would we all start talking about it and questioning what was going on. Ross would come over to the house and start saying all these strange things about what he was going to do to his old boss. Like one day, he came over to see me, and as we were sitting there talking about this and that, all of a sudden, Ross looked at me and said that he was going to get a gun and kill his old boss. "Are you kidding me?" I said. "You know that I could call the police right now and report you for talking that way." He just looked at me with this dumbfounded look on his face, then I knew something was terribly wrong. He would tell us that he was going to get some jobs on his computer to work from home. He would also tell us that he had given out his Visa number to get the job he wanted, so they took over $6,000 out of the card. He would say that they would pay him back all the money after he got paid. When we told him it was a scam, he got so upset with all of us. We stopped talking to him about it, but we did not stop talking to each other. Something was going on, and we all could see it and tell what it was.

Joe had his six-month appointment with Dr. Quinn in July up at OHSU clinic. During that appointment, I was telling Dr. Quinn about how odd Ross was starting to act, saying how, funny, it was almost like he had Alzheimer's like Joe. But it could also be stress because he just lost his job.

Dr. Quinn gave me this funny look, and his eyes got big, then he said, "I want to see him on Joe's next appointment. Tell him to get his VA card [veterans affairs], and let us know if anything happens."

Ross is the father of two young daughters in their late teens and early twenties and the grandfather to one little boy. He been divorced for a long time; that was why I stepped in to help, because I had already been through this. He was looking for jobs, just like Joe did, also having a hard time writing up and comprehending résumés and job applications.

Then one day he called me to say that he had a job interview, but it would be out of town. (I was happy for him, but out of town?)

He took the job. They had some class, and he had to go back east for orientation. He would be gone for three to four days. "Okay, I hope it all works out for you," I said. After the second day he was home, I talked to him about everything that went down. He said that it wasn't the job he thought it was, and they had a lot to go through.

My instinct told me that it was hard to remember everything, just like Joe had gone through. I did feel sorry for Ross because he was all alone in this. The girls were there, but they were so young, and one already had a child, so I helped them both try to figure out what they should do. So he was back looking for a new job. During this time, my friend Cathi, who was a real estate agent for Windermere, was talking to Ross about his home. She knew all about Joe and his disease. She told Ross not to worry as the two of us would help him in selling his house and getting everything taken care of.

On February 7, 2012, it was Joe's six-month appointment, so the two of us were going to go back up to see Dr. Quinn. This time, Ross, with Jackie, a friend of ours, was going too. I did not want to be up there all by myself with the two of them. Sometimes it is just so hard even with one of them, so Jackie stayed with Ross while Joe and I went in for his appointment. I told Dr. Quinn that Ross was out in the waiting room. He gave me that look again! After Joe's appointment was over, we all came out to the waiting room. Dr. Quinn stopped at the receptionist desk and told them to push back all his patients back thirty minutes.

I introduced Ross to Dr. Quinn, and the two of them walked off together. Jackie looked at me. All she could say was "There is something going on with him." She could see it also, but neither one of us wanted to say the word. About thirty minutes after the two of them walked out, Ross took a seat next to Joe, and Dr. Quinn asked if he could please speak to me.

THE LOVE OF MY LIFE

Do you know when you get that sinking feeling that something bad is about to happen?

We walked to a corner of the waiting room. "Mrs. Michaud, it doesn't look good," he said. "I'd like to see him again in about a week for a blood work up, a CT scan."

Great, two brothers with this disease.

What fun for me, I get to go home and tell his daughters and brother and the whole damn family that he had Alzheimer's also! I got them all together so we could talk about what he was going to have to do and what they were all going to have to do.

We discussed and decided it was time for Cathi to put Ross's house on the market, and then after that, Ross and Erika would move into a bigger apartment together for the time being. Ross's house sold on March 2012! We had a huge garage sale for him. Cathi and her friend and I worked it for four days. He kept wanting to give everything away for free. He was also a huge woodworker and a machinist. We had to call in a special person to tell us what cost we should ask for.

He moved into an apartment with Erika, which turned out to be a difficult thing for the two of them. Ross did not want to give up his belongings, even though he had a garage sale; if it didn't sell, he was taking it with him, even though he had a lot of other belongings of his own to bring. Then there was all of Erika's things too.

We all helped them move into the apartment, but we also tried to keep Ross occupied so we could move things in and out of the storage shed and the apartment into cars and trucks to take to the goodwill for Erika. (The man had a lot of stuff.)

I went with Erika to one of Ross's first appointment with Dr. Quinn, just to help her out a little. They did all the normal stuff that Dr. Quinn would normally do at their first visit, with all the testing and everything. Then we got a big, big surprise. He looked at Ross and then at us and said that he should no longer drive. Oh my god, not again.

Can I say that it went over like a lead balloon, just like Joe's did. Also, let me tell you, he got so mad that he was telling all of us that he would be driving his car, and no one would be stopping him.

First, we tried to talk to him about what could possibly happen, but he would hear none of that. All he knew was that Erika was his youngest daughter, who was trying to take his driving license away from him. He would not have anything to do with it, and under no circumstances was anyone taking his driver's license away.

You have to know one thing here: Ross has raised his two girls by himself for over twelve years since his divorce. He was still coherent enough to know that he was the father, so every time Erika tried to tell him something that he didn't like or want to hear, his fathering instincts kicked in, and he tried to put her back in her place. But when it comes to me, I'm an adult, his sister-in-law, who married his oldest brother. So I wouldn't put up with a lot of his outburst, and he knew it.

Thank God I drove my car, but the two of them were screaming at each other all the way. Erika was crying, and I was crying just remembering everything I had to go through with Joe. I could see this was not going to go anywhere, so I tossed him his keys, told him to drive home. The look on Erika's face was priceless. I told Ross to call me when he got home so I would know that he made it home safely.

I told Erika, "It is going to be okay. This is what we are going to do now. We are going to go over to Bi-Mart to buy a steering wheel lock, then you call one of your friends to put it on the steering wheel. So that way, you will not be lying to him when he accuses you of doing it, and we all know that he will.

"Also, look for all the car keys when he's in the shower. That way, he won't see you snooping through his things and get truly upset with you. Because they get to a point where they start hiding things. Have one of your friends take all the keys out of the house, because he will be going through all of your things in the whole apartment, looking for them."

After a time, things went smoothly with the car, but then there were other problems that came up like normal. So we would talk on the phone a lot about what was going on and what to expect. Erika would make out a grocery list, then the two of them would go grocery shopping. She would ask her father what he would like to have for dinner and what they would like to buy. Sometimes he would throw a fit, saying, "You never buy or cook anything I like, so why do we go grocery shopping?"

The sad thing was that I already put my husband in a care facility with this disease called Alzheimer's. Now I was going through the same trial and tribulations like I did before, trying to help my niece Erika, who was in her early twenties, understand the disease. Her older sister didn't want to have anything to do with her father or her sister, which pertains to her father. So Erika was on her own. She was a smart young woman, and I had all the faith in her. She also had Tony, Ross's baby brother, and me to help her anytime, to talk to.

But with this horrible disease, Alzheimer's, it can kick your butt from here to kingdom come and back without even knowing it. It also will take the youngest of caregivers too.

This is what Erika had to say back in 2013:

I am exhausted . . . I am full of plenty of lovely emotions. I hate this disease, it's really, really hard, and I'm struggling. But I'm fine. Dad is attempting to sell his car to my aunt's son or something for $500 because he is family. I told him that will not happen, because we will need the money. I know how much care facilities cost. I'm starting to save now. Dad needs to as well, yet he doesn't understand this, obviously. The car is locked with the club, so obviously he cannot drive it away without me being there to approve. And he is not happy about it.

Paying bills is extremely difficult. He doesn't want to give me the password to *anything*, so I have to sneak on his computer or call over the phone every month. When he's out of the house long enough, I will copy it all down so I won't have to do that anymore.

I need to find him a babysitter. I have to work 8:00 a.m. to 4:00 p.m. Monday to Friday, and I want someone around.

The lawyer whom I have been trying to contact about the whole $6,000 Visa thing has been out of the office for two months.

Amy and I aren't talking. I knew it was a matter of time. She told me that I *deserve* to have to take care of our dad all on my own.

I know I haven't exactly asked for help, but at the same time, I feel isolated. No one else is going through this with me. Except my aunt Pat, and she is doing all she can to take care of Uncle Joe. No one is ever here, no one else takes care of him.

No one calls him. This apartment is like my trap. Because wherever I go, he is here. Whenever I come home, he's here. We can't spend five minutes in the same room before he picks a fight. Everything is an argument. It's hard for me to reach out to people. It makes me feel weak. I don't want to have to do this all on my own.

We visited the VA Hospital last Friday to speak with a speech pathologist. My dad didn't understand any part of the visit. She gave me lots of information about day trips and camps that other patients of hers have loved.

By February 2013, Ross was placed onto Pacifica Senior Living, the same place Joe was at; they were also in the same cottage 1. Joe was already acclimated to being here since it's been two years for him. But Ross was **not** acclimated at all to living here. It took him a long, long time to get acclimated. He downright got mean for a time.

He would try to break down the doors or break through a window or two. One day he got out of the cottage, and he started to run. They got to him in the main lobby, where they ended up closing all the doors and keeping all of the residents' guests to come in through the back entry. He was having a standoff with them—not talking, not moving, no nothing. I just happened to be coming in to see Joe through one of the other doors and found Ross sitting in the front door waiting area. I asked him what was going on. I tried to talk to him, but he was so out of control and angry you could not even redirect him.

One of the caregivers told me, as long as he did not hit or tried to injure anyone, they would not have to call the police. So we all sat there till he could calm down so they could walk him back into the cottage.

He was not happy about going back into the cottage, but they did get him in there. Funny thing is that Joe and all the other gentlemen did not pay any attention to all the commotion going on.

Like all the residents, Ross himself started a routine and was doing quite well there. They all knew that they got three meals a day plus two snacks a day. They got to go on outings, with activities, with a place for them to walk, and boy, did he enjoy his walking, just like Joe. Ross was a much faster walker than Joe was. Joe could not keep up with him.

They would always sit by each other during dinner or in the common area, watching TV. John would always be by Joe's side too. After a period of time, Joe didn't really know who Ross was; he just knew that he was someone important to him and would smile now and then at him. It made it easier on Ross, and all of us also, that I went to see Joe every day. So Ross could come and sit with me and visit, knowing that someone was there for him too.

CHAPTER 10

Thoughts on My Brothers

**by
Tony Michaud**

Driving at night, you tend to have a lot of time just to think about life without the distractions of other traffic, scenery, and Qualcomm messaging you every so often with questions from dispatchers, safety announcements, and whatnot. Especially when you are driving at 3:00 a.m.

This was the case the other day as I had to make a delivery today and to set up for my appointment time. I needed to do some late-night driving. I often did my best thinking at 3:00 a.m., whether after a night out at a bar or sitting on the toilet, but that's another blog.

The subject of my thoughts for this morning was my brothers, my oldest brother, Joe, and my older brother, Ross, and my "sister" Pat.

Joe was diagnosed with Alzheimer's a number of years ago. His wife, Pat, took care of him for all those years, essentially giving up her own ambitions to tend to his needs, walk him through the maze of social agencies, doctors, hospitals, and therapies to give quality to his life. She put up with a lot—a ton. None of which I will enumerate here as I feel his privacy and hers are just that, private. Just let it be sufficient to say that she put her life on hold to make sure that his was good.

I thank her for that and, among other things, love her very much for doing what she did; she is on par with Sister Teresa for what she did and, through action, showed how much she loves my brother.

Three or four years ago, I saw how it was starting to tear her up. She could no longer go to work (another love of her life), had to limit vacations, and was now attached at the hip with my brother. Her quality of life was going down with each level Joe's disease was attacking him. I had finally seen enough and begged her to put him into a care facility. She didn't, couldn't; it wasn't in her ability. She felt that not caring for her husband was a mortal sin. I nagged her for a long time, gave her all the arguments I could, but she wouldn't give up.

Finally, last year, she finally relented and put Joe in a care facility. He is doing great, has lots of friends, is in a routine, and that helps with his disease. But his disease is still worsening. The last time I was home and saw him, he had forgotten my name, and it took a little time for him to recognize me. He no longer knows Pat's name and barely remembers being married to her.

Alzheimer's is a motherfucker.

It will attack the afflicted but kill the spouse who cares for the patient because of the stress of caring for the afflicted. It's all collateral damage. That's why I begged Pat to put Joe in a facility.

Ross, my other brother, was diagnosed with Alzheimer's just a few weeks ago. The family had its suspicions. Ross has been having a problem with his memory for the past few years, and recently, it has been getting really bad. He has also started withdrawing, another symptom of the disease.

My niece Erika, Ross's daughter, has given up her life to share an apartment with him. She is young, just turned twenty-one this last year, and has a lot of life still to live. With her too there will be a point that she must give up and put him into a care facility. She is too young to give up her youth to an old-age disease, and I hope that when the time comes, she will see the wisdom in what has to be done.

And again, Pat, who has seen this all before and is a veteran of dealing with this disease, has once again stepped up to the plate to help Erica with the maze of social programs, doctors, hospitals, and whatnot.

She is truly an angel. They both are.

My whole point to this story is that I miss my brothers, and that is what I was thinking about the other night at 3:00 a.m. I miss the camaraderie of our youth, the jokes and gentle chiding at family get-togethers, the disdain of Joe when I got yet another low-pay job, the shoulder of Ross when my heart ached.

We never really hung around together much, but when the chips were down, you could always count on them. They were the last line of defense and the first to let you know you were doing it wrong.

That's what big brothers are for, and they did a marvelous job. And now, even though they may not have passed away, I have lost them to a terrible, terrible disease. And I miss them.

CHAPTER 11

What, Parkinson's Too?

Joe's right hand always did a little shake, but the further he got into the disease, it got a lot worse. Now his whole body was shaking. It wasn't just shaking; he would jerk almost out of his wheelchair sometimes. So Memo, the head caregiver, in cottage 5, with the nurses for Pacifica, also the nurse for hospice, and I all got together to talk about what to do for him, so we started to look at his medication to figure out which one he really didn't need or to eliminate or cut back on some of them so we could see what the outcome would be. Hopefully it would subside some of his shaking.

This was all going on in mid-June of 2014. The kids and I had already planned a year ago to do a vacation about this time. So on the twenty-fifth of June, we rented a car, plus having Buddy's pick up, we all headed off to Whidbey Island, in Washington. There we would hook up with Buddy's parents, Tony and Doreen, who flew in from Manchester, New Hampshire, for a few days. After we had spent time up there, Cortney and my grandsons, Gage and JW, with me headed east for North Dakota to a little town called Starkweather. All four of us were going back for a family reunion on my dad's side.

Then off to Devil's Lake for about twelve days. Can I say, everyone needs to take a vacation from time to time. Again, with all the stress that you're under and the care to a loved one that you provide, you need to take care of yourselves. It's not that you will forget them. You will definitely will miss them, but you also need to keep an eye on your own self.

I would always call in to check on him, to see how his days were going or to see if he needed anything, but they would always tell me that he was doing fine, and there was no change. Sometimes I would not know if that was good or bad.

Just knowing that he was being taken care of by responsible people that cared for him meant a whole hell of a lot to me. So that gives you a chance to relax and enjoy your vacation.

While we were gone, one of the doctors from Gentiva decided to make a care center visit to see what all the nurses were talking about regarding Joe's shaking and jerking. I guess with what he thought could be a diagnosis to what was going on with Joe.

I received the phone call one afternoon from Memo, telling me that a Gentiva hospice doctor had been there to see Joe, with a diagnosis of the possibility of Parkinson's disease coming on. Just sitting there with the phone up to my ears, I was starting to get heart palpitations, my breathing was changing, and my head was ringing. All I remember saying to myself over and over again was *What more is he going to have to endure? He's gone down so far now.* Thank God we were on the road tomorrow. I told Memo I would see him in two days.

The day I got home, I went right over to see Joe, to check him out myself, to make sure everything was okay with him. I also got a hold of all the nurses to read the report that the doctor had put in Joe's binder. Then I put a call into Dr. Quinn and told the nurses up there that he needed to call me ASAP. I also knew that Dr. Quinn had moved to the Parkinson's disease research department up at OHSU, so this could help us out a lot. **(I hoped.)** Joe had dropped some weight while I was gone, and he had also refused to eat, which we knew was difficult for him. In the later stage, they forget how to swallow. So this meant a huge, big drop. It just occurred.

I also knew that Memo and the other caregivers had started moving his wheelchair sideways at the dining room table. So when he did one of his major jerks, he didn't hit his knees or hands, so he wouldn't bruise them up so bad. Also to stop him from knocking everything off the table.

THE LOVE OF MY LIFE

I received a phone call from Dr. Quinn. You know, it's nice to have a great rapport with your doctor. Also to know that he truly cares about his patients. I filled him in on everything that was going on because he hadn't seen Joe for quite a while, like, maybe over a year, as it was a little difficult for me to bring him up there to see him.

I would have to get the caregiver van and also a caregiver to go with me. So I normally would talk to him on the phone anyway. Even though I would talk to him about what was going on in my life, I would keep him abreast of Joe and Ross at all times. We talked about all the big changes in Joe, and especially the new jerking and how bad they were getting.

Dr. Quinn wanted to see him, but he also knew it would be hard for me too. So he told me that we would be doing a house call, or is it a care center call?

Hell, whatever you call it, he was coming to see Joe.

How many doctors that you know of would still make the effort to make a house call this day and age? Not a whole hell of a lot.

So thank you, Dr. Quinn, for being there for Joe.

So we made the appointment; it would be on the twenty-fifth of July at about 3:00 p.m. in cottage 5; that way, he could look in on the two of them at the same time. Also by leaving his office around 2:30 p.m., he hoped he wouldn't get into all the rush hour traffic from OHSU. He got to the care center probably around 3:30 p.m. and said that the traffic wasn't too bad. Joe was sitting in his wheelchair, like always, in the common area, and I was sitting on a couch right next to him, like always. I was watching TV, while Joe was staring straight at the ceiling because his eyes were developing tunnel vision. Dr. Quinn made his way over to us and sat on the arm of one of the rocking chairs.

We talked for a bit about this and that, then he started to do his diagnoses of the problem or possibility that was going on with Joe. He could see that Joe's right hand was shaking, but he'd seen that before. He had diagnosed it before and had written it down in all of Joe's records. Then Joe did one of his big jerks; that one took

Dr. Quinn by surprise. He looked at me and asked, "How long has he been doing this?" He did a little more of an examination on Joe.

"So is it Parkinson's disease or what?" I needed to know.

I thought to myself, *I do not know if I could go through much more, let alone have Joe go through much more too.* Dr. Quinn looked at me and said, "No, it is not Parkinson's, but what it is called is mild fraction impairment. Which means his brain is kind of short-circuiting and sending shock waves through him. There really isn't a lot we can do for him. It's the disease taking a hold of his brain."

"Great that's all he needs now."

After that, we walked to cottage 1 to see Ross, where we found him sitting, watching TV. Ross looked at me and smiled. He knew who I was. But then he looked over at Dr. Quinn, not quite sure of who he was. So I introduced them to each other and said to him, "You know who this person is? Up on Pill Hill, you and Joe both go to him. This is Dr. Quinn." He did a small examination on Ross and could see that his right hand was also starting to shake like Joe's did in the early stages of this disease Alzheimer's.

We also noticed that he was becoming more of an introvert. Because he really didn't like to socialize with anyone and stuck to himself all the time, even in a cottage of thirteen or so residents. Dr. Quinn said that he looked good, but only time would tell.

After everything was said and done, we walked outside. Dr. Quinn told me that he knew the doctor from Gentiva, so he could read Joe's report. He would get ahold of him to discuss Joe's diagnosis. As we stood there, I looked at him and asked point-blank, "How much longer does Joe have to live?" Which I knew he couldn't say or really know at this point, but I was going to try anyway. "How much further are they supposed to go before they can't go any further?" He just looked at me with his kind face and shook his head and said, "Probably a year or less."

During this time, I started to see a bereavement coordinator, by the name of Jack, through Gentiva hospice. We would need either at the care facility, or he would drop by the house. Just speaking to someone about what was going to happen, what was going to change in our life, and how to react to certain things did help me a lot. Also just knowing that there was someplace I could go to meet other people in the same situation as I was going through did help.

You know this is going to go that one way, and your heart and soul knows that too. But you cannot see it that way. All you can do is pray for it not to come.

CHAPTER 12

How to Say Good-bye

Dr. Quinn was right; it was less than a month.

It had been one of those months, starting with the middle of July. With three funerals already in July and one already in August. All these gentlemen were either ex-coworkers when he worked at Fred Meyers or ham radio operators who became friends that he'd known for a long time or just very good friends. I was getting to a point where I couldn't take it anymore, going to all these funerals, thinking about my own husband's funeral and what it would do to me and the girls.

So I was so happy to be one of the Red Hatters, having a big sister group of good friends where we could do a lot of things together. That Sunday on August 17, I was up early, getting everything ready. Just working in the backyard, getting ready for a pool party for all my Red Hat sisters.

But all I knew was that I really needed to see Joe for some reason. I was there at lunchtime like always on Saturday. He was quiet, but he was in good spirits for as good as you can get for him. I held his hand, and I talked to him. They also had some old fifties classic music on the radio, so I sang to him some of the oldies but goodies ones I liked. Which you truly do not want to hear me sing. All I knew was that the two of us were together and happy. He had a good lunch, and he drank about three glasses of juice and water for me. Which was good considering he didn't want to eat or drink anything there for a while. After about two or three hours, I said good-bye, kissed him like always, and told him I loved him with all my heart and said, "I'll see you tomorrow sometime."

I knew that they were about to put him back to bed so he could rest up and make him comfortable after sitting in the chair for so long.

I knew on Saturday night I was really overly tired, so I went to bed early. I knew that I tossed and turned, got up and down until about 3:00 a.m.

I couldn't get Joe out of my mind. I kept thinking of him. I knew they would call me if anything was going wrong; they always did.

Finally and happily, I got some sleep, but not a lot. I was up at six. I was sitting, finishing my cup of coffee, thinking about what to have for breakfast. But still thinking about Joe all this time. You know when you get that feeling that something's not quite right, but you're not quite sure what it is. Then all of a sudden, the phone rang, which scared the crap out of me. I looked at the clock, and it was only nine thirty in the morning.

It was Adele, the nurse on duty at the Pacifica. "Pat, I need to tell you that Joe is not doing very well. I believe you need to get in here as soon as you can."

She also said that they had called hospice too; they were on their way. My heart stopped, and all I could say was "I'll be there as soon as I can." I had to at least wash my face and get dressed. One thing about me is when I need to get someplace fast, I do know how to put the pedal to the metal. I lived on 12. All I had to do was get to 182nd. So by God, every car better stay out of my way. This was my husband, my life I was thinking about. I needed to get to him and be there with him. I tried to call Cortney and Morgan on their cell phone, but no one would pick up. It was a Sunday morning; either they were sleeping in or they had already gotten up for the day to do something fun.

All I knew was this was not a message I wanted to leave on their phones. So all I said was "Please call me right away." By the time I got there, they already started him on morphine every thirty minutes and lorazepam every four hours.

The girls started to call in. I had to tell them that they had to get here. It did not look good for their dad. Cortney was out for a run, so she and her boys stopped running, and they got here first. But Morgan lived up in Ellensburg, Washington, about a four-hour drive away from us. As I sat there, talking to all the nurses from Pacifica and hospice, watching Joe breathe in and out, and thinking about our life together, I knew that this was going to be a very long day. I told Pacifica a long time ago, if anything ever happened to Joe or we got to the point where we knew he was going to pass, I would be moving into his room to be with him for as long as it took. I knew they believed me, with Joe being there for so long.

With Cortney there, we started to talk and make a list of all our families and friends to call. We also knew which ones could do a phone tree list, which would help us out immensely. Joe's brother Tony came in with Ross's youngest daughter, Erika. Family and friends started to call or drop by, but I really didn't want to see anyone. My concern was more on Joe and the girls at this time. Morgan got there about 3:00 p.m. Poor thing, what a long drive when you think that you may not see your dad again. She walked in, and you could tell that this was going to be very rough on her. Because the last time she saw her father, it was only for a very short time, one day in January.

Morgan's daughter, Elly May, my then four-year-old granddaughter, walked over to where he was lying. Looking at him, she put her fingers to her mouth and went "Shhhhhhhhh, Papa is sleeping." We all watched him as the day went into night. It grew longer with every breath he took. I asked Cortney to please go to the house and pick up some things for me that I would need to stay for a while and bring them back. Because I knew I definitely was not leaving him. Also to take Reno, my golden retriever, to her house for me.

The caregivers came and went with the medication rotating and just seeing if they could do anything to help us. Friends and family were bringing in all kinds of food and drinks for everyone to have, but for me, I was not hungry; all I wanted to do was be by Joe's side. I started to send everybody home. Morgan's little ones had already left with a good friend that afternoon. But the girls wanted to stay, and I told them no, they needed to go to get sleep.

"I'll be here if anything happens. I'll call you." Sorry to say, but truly I was just happy to have everyone leave Joe's room. Since everybody started coming in this morning, I hadn't had one moment alone with him, and I needed that time to be with him. I curled up in Harry's bed, one of the resident that shared a room with Joe. I didn't get much sleep, knowing that my husband was dying in the bed next to me, and with all the crying I was doing, sleep was out of the question. Then with all the staff coming in and out to do meds, rotating him, and just seeing how we all were doing.

Monday was the same as Sunday, with more people coming and going or just calling in to see how he was doing and if there was anything they could do for us. Sitting there, watching him having to go through this, knowing that I could not do a damn thing to help.

I could see he was in so much pain; he would grimace, with a pained look on his face all the time, even though he had been semi-unconscious the whole time. He was starting also to go into the fetal position. They would come in and rotate him, and then they would massage his legs to make him more comfortable. You could see him relax because he would begin to snore, and that was a good sign that his mind was letting him relax a little.

There would be times when I didn't want them to rotate him because of the look on his face. I didn't want him to be in any more pain. Also with my stress level at its highest, I shouted out, "Why do you have to always do things like this to him, can't you see he's dying?" I knew they cared for him and was only helping all of us out. With this disease, it's like a crap shoot in which way they will die. I have seen it all here. Sometimes they just relax and go to sleep or go into a coma. Joe would be there, but not there, kinda like being in a coma but still suffering and feeling all the pain but couldn't do anything about it before he passed.

On Monday night, Cortney called the church they belonged to and asked if one of the fathers could come in and give Joe his last rites because he was having such a difficult time. We knew he wasn't going to last much longer. Father John came about 8:00 p.m. that night.

He was happy to help us and Joe out with the last rites and gave him his blessings. We also did a prayer for him too. Father John said we could call him if we needed anything else.

After the girls went home and I was getting ready for bed, if that were possible; it was about 10:30 p.m. There was a knock on the door. People were always coming and going all day long. It was maybe one of them, but no, it was not. I opened the door, and there stood a great friend of ours, Pam. She just looked at me and said, "I'm here for the whole night." I didn't quite understand what she said. She could see that I was getting ready for bed. I just looked around the room, like, where are you going to sleep? She came in and put her bag down and said that she would be spending the night here in a chair so I could get some needed rest and not have to be jumping up and down all night with Joe.

Pam did stay up all night long, watching Joe and watching TV a little. Good thing they all had cable TV there. But I was up and down anyway. I did get some sleep, thanks to her.

Tuesday rolled in, and Joe was still hanging in there, but the pain, as I could see, was getting worse. He was also starting to curl up into a fetal position. The caregivers were having a hard time straightening him out.

He was so tense, and it was hard to watch them trying to rotate him, which caused him more pain and me more stress. At this point, what difference did it make. Leaving him in the fetal position helped him to breathe and be comfortable. We had talked about stopping all the rotating, because that put him in too much pain. I also knew that they did not want him to have bed sores. We are talking end of life here, possibly hours left, so we all came to an understanding; they would rotate every four hours instead of every two.

> *What was he going to do, take the bed sores with him? I didn't think so.*

You could tell it was getting harder and harder for him to breathe. The girls and I stayed right there by his side at all times.

Morgan was behind him, Cortney was at his feet and side, and as for me, I was always right by his head.

On Tuesday afternoon, hospice brought in a harpist, who would play comforting music. The harpist focuses on the patient's breathing and will plays music by the way they are breathing. Because of the way I myself and the girls were surrounding him, she could not see his breathing. Therefore, she played to our crying and breathing, which surprisingly brought us a great deal of comfort.

Ann, the hospice chaplain, said she wishes she had a camera; she said it was absolutely beautiful, with the girls and me lying next to him. All three of us happened to have on gray sweatshirts that day. So as the harpist played, it was peaceful.

I had not left Joe's side since being there since Sunday morning, so by Tuesday afternoon, Jackie and all the rest of the family decided that it was time that I left the room to get some air and also to clear my head. Jackie walked up to me later and put her hand on my shoulder and said, "All of us believe you need to go outside just for the time being and get some fresh air."

"No, I don't want to leave his side," I kept saying. "In case something happens to him while I'm outside."

But finally I did go outside to the back courtyard, where they had a beautiful gazebo. Tony and I sat there, reminiscing about Joe and Ross, taking in what a beautiful day it was. "Okay," I said, "time to go in." Tony looked at his watch and said, "We've only been out here for ten minutes."

Okay by me. When we were walking back into the common area, Jackie came out of Joe's room with a look of panic on her face.

"Oh my god, he died," I said.

She had to grab me because I almost went to the floor. In a panic state, my knees always give way first. Because that was one of my biggest fears, that I would be out of the room when Joe passed. "No," she had to say, "he's still with us. His breathing changed a little bit, so I wanted to come and get you." After that, we all walked back into the room. I would not leave his side after that.

People were still bringing us food all the time. The kitchen there at Pacifica always brought us pots of coffee with pastries. Sorry, but when I get stressed out, I do not like to eat. So about 8:00 p.m. on Tuesday night, Tony had this great idea. He said he was going to get me something to eat. Whatever it was, it didn't matter. How far he had to go, it didn't matter also. But he would do it. We argued back and forth about this. I decided, okay, fine. I thought for a time about what could make him go and get off my back for some time. I had it. I love popcorn with real butter on it, the ones you get in the theaters. Thinking this would take him awhile, he just smiled at me, saying "OK." He got up and said, "If that's what you want, that's what you'll get."

Off he went. About thirty minutes after he left, he walked back into the room, carrying with him two huge buckets of my favorite buttered popcorn. From the theater house down the street. "Okay," he said, "enjoy," and we did.

There just happen to be five of us in Joe's room: Cortney, Morgan, Jackie, Pam, and of course, me. All of us were going to be spending the night with him there. Cortney made a joke, saying that her dad was pimping tonight with all five of us ladies. We all laughed at that, knowing Joe would be laughing too.

It had already been a rough two days since Sunday morning, with Joe not once opening his eyes or realizing any of us were there. With him moaning in pain, trying to keep him comfortable was all we could do for him. So to be able to laugh a little and have some light liberty made everyone more comfortable.

I knew Joe so well that he would not want us to sit around and mope or cry like we all were doing but instead to enjoy the evening and reminisce, laugh, and play cards if we had them. So he could hear us for one last time, enjoying just being a family. I truly believe that was the kind of person he truly was, and he would not want to make this any more difficult as it already was.

We all tried to get comfortable for the night, knowing it was going to be hard on all of us. Two of us tried to sleep in a twin bed, which was definitely difficult to start with. Two in chairs that were too small, one on the floor. Can I say, we all did not get any sleep at all. The nice part of the evening was that they upped Joe's morphine for him.

They would come in every fifteen to thirty minutes to check on him. His breathing was starting to labor. He was also drowning from the inside. All the water was closing around his lungs and heart. It was getting harder and harder to give him his medication.

They had to start using a syringe, but they had to be careful. They could not put it between his teeth as he would clamp down on it. And we all would be afraid that he would bite it or break it. So they started to use the side of his mouth closest to the inside of his cheek.

About 4:00 a.m. on Wednesday morning, one of the night caregivers came in to give Joe his morphine. He stuck it in by his cheek. He must have put it in a little too fast, because within five minutes, Joe was throwing up. All of us ran to his side, rolling him on to the side of the bed to let everything drain out of his nose and mouth. I do not know who called for help, but the caregivers came running. It took some time to get him back to being comfortable, as comfortable as they could get him. They tried some more morphine and gave it to him real slow.

The three of us girls got into our normal position with him, Morgan behind him, Cortney at his side, and me always by his head. It was about 7:30 a.m., and Joe's breathing was becoming labored even more; he was now holding his breath then letting it out slowly. We were all starting to get a little panicky.

How do you tell your beloved of forty-two years that you love him so deeply that it is all right for him to go? "Go to your mom and dad, they're waiting for you. The girls and I will be just fine. All I want is for you to be back to who you should be, healthy and happy again. That's all." Knowing that my heart was breaking in two, also knowing I would never see him again, touch him or kiss him or just talk to him.

His breathing was getting shallower and shallower, and then finally that last breath came. Joe's eyes opened, and they were so clear. ***"Oh god, please let him know that I was here with him, and let him know how much I love him."***

My beloved husband died on August 20, 2014, at 8:30 a.m. What was I going to do now without him? I told everybody to please leave the room. I wanted my time alone with him, after all. After a period of time, they told me it was time to go.

All I wanted was to be by his side, to stay with him, but I also knew all of Joe's wishes. All the hospice people were going to get Joe ready for Mount Scott Funeral Home, because they were coming to get him. They were going to transport him up to OHSH Research Center. Where Joe wanted to donate his brain to science. He wanted to help stop this deadly disease Alzheimer's, even if that meant donating his brain and anything else that they wanted that would help out. I received a phone call while Joe was up at OHSU. They asked if it was possible for them to take part of his stomach for research as well. I told them to please take whatever they could for research and whatever they could that they could possibly donate, like his eyes, maybe.

The girls and I knew we were going to have a long week ahead of us, getting everything ready for his service. Thank God I had already taken care of all the arrangements for him.

Losing someone you love is hard enough, and then having to go through all the burial procedure, it's like losing them all over again. The service was very nice, from what I could remember of it. They did a full military honors for him.

Thank you to the Patriot Guard Riders for supporting our heroes.

After everything is done and everybody's left, you start to calculate what this whole disease has cost you.

Besides losing the love of my life, it cost us all of Joe's 401K, his MetLife Insurance, his retirement, and the savings.

The sad thing was that I was going to have to start all over on a lot of things. Thank God I had my 401K and my MetLife. This was a truly rude awakening and a hard reality check for me and everybody else that would be diagnosed.

CHAPTER 13

Who Am I Now?

Who am I now?

That's so funny. Who have I been? I don't even know myself either. All I know is that for the last eleven years, I have tried to do my best and take good care of my husband and myself. Yes, I worked some until it got to a point where I was so worried about Joe all the time, and it was so hard on the both of us all the time. Then I tried part-time jobs, and that didn't help us either; it only helped me out by keeping me in the workforce, with people I could talk to. But with Joe always getting lost on his walks and with him not liking to be at home alone, that really put me in a bind.

Eleven years of doing the same routine can grate on your nerves, even though you are doing it for a loved one. But the funny thing is, Joe has passed away, and I'm still doing the same routine. I wish I had a trade or skill to fall back on. My parents, God rest their souls, never once talked to us kids about going to college. I guess it was because they were both raised on farms back then. Daddy in North Dakota in a little town called Stark Weather, and Mom lived in Illinois. All I know is at a certain age, Daddy packed up and moved to Oregon for work, while Mom went straight into the Army after high school. At one time, I was thinking about going into the Air Force, but the guy I was dating at that time was coming out of the Army, and he talked me out of it. Which was kind of good and bad, but then I would have never met Joe.

Please don't get me wrong, I had a wonderful life, a fantastic marriage. To a person whom I loved with all my heart and soul. We were so happy being together.

We also had two beautiful daughters and four grandchildren. All I know is that when Joe was diagnosed, I was only fifty-two, and now I'm sixty-four.

A whole decade of my life disappeared, so I'm not quite sure who I am or what I'm supposed to do now.

I know I love being with my grandchildren; they always make me laugh, and they also keep my mind off thinking of Joe so much. But at nighttime, oh, the nights are the ones that are the worst for me. You can watch mindless TV or just keep flipping through the TV shows to a point where you don't care anymore.

How many times can you play on your computer till it gets so monotonous? Then when you do go off to bed, all you do is cry, because the memories of your husband are so strong, and the bed is so big. You do have a lifetime of great memories together, and you try to keep all the happy ones alive with you. But the sad ones keep creeping into your mind and heart also. And I believe those are the ones that haunt you the most.

All your family and friends have families, with their own lives to live. You can't keep bothering them to go to lunch or just to talk to or even just to have someone there. I know I just want to be with someone.

You also know you have to start living your own life alone, but that's so hard to do after having someone there by your side for all those years.

I truly believe this is why I wanted to start writing this book. One, to keep all the memories of Joe alive in me and remember what I learned and went through in these eleven years with this disease they call Alzheimer's, also for all the love I had for my husband.

I believe most of all, I would very much like to be able to help other people who are in the same predicament that I was in. Who have a loved one whom they believe is getting ill or has already been diagnosed with Alzheimer's. Just to be able to understand all the signs, to be able to cope with all the good and the bad, that can be a big help.

For me, I know I'll make it. It will be difficult, but not as difficult as what Joe went through. Because if Joe could struggle through it and be strong, then I could be too. Watching him, Joe has taught me a lot. He is the one who made me stronger than I ever thought I could be. With all I have learned and been through with this wretched disease, it has made me into the person that I am today.

I'll be taking it one step at a time. Moving too fast is not a great idea. I've had to learn the hard way. Once I placed Joe in the care facility, I started thinking about selling the house, where we had lived for over thirty-nine years and where we raised our daughters. There are truly a lot of great memories here, good ones and some bad ones too. I also know not to do anything for a good year or two.

So who am I now, only God knows. I know he has a plan for me. I may not know what it is, I also wish I did know what it is, but it is out there—that, I do know. So as of today, it is a day-by-day existence. I also know I'm going to have some good days and some bad ones. With lots of ups and downs in between too.

I just lost the love of my life. I also know that Joe would not want me to give up. He would want me to move on with life too. I have a great core group of friends whom I rely on deeply, also with the help from my daughters, grandkids, and my new golden retriever, Reno.

I also know everything will not come together in the blink of an eye, but it will come together someday and sometime. All you have to do is hope and pray that everything will work out for the best.

I also know that I'm not the only one out there going through this; this I know for a fact. During the months of June through September of 2014, I had six friends lose their spouses. It wasn't a very good year.

I'm starting a new chapter in my life now. It's been over a year since Joe passed away. Some things are okay, some things are not so okay, but I'm keeping busy, doing a lot of things to help. I'm doing some traveling with Diane. Diane's husband, Vern, was one of Joe's best friends, and the two of them were our traveling companions.

Vern died exactly twenty-four hours after Joe did. He had been battling cancer for quite a while. Sorry to say that the cancer finally won. We will all truly miss you, Vern, and you will always be loved forever. God bless you, and rest in peace. You two have a great time together.

So working on this book has helped me immensely. It kept me going with what life was throwing at me. Nights are still the hardest, but I know they're going to get easier. All you can do is keep on trudging on, with the knowledge that someday you will see your loved one again.

For the time being, I'll keep busy volunteering at the elementary school, being a scorekeeper for JW's baseball team, and traveling up to Ellensburg with Reno to see Morgan and my two youngest grandchildren. Life will be good, and life will move on.

God bless each and every one of you who have lost a spouse, a parent, or a loved one to this wretched disease they call Alzheimer's.

CHAPTER 14

Eulogy to Joe

By Tony Michaud

When I was eight or nine, my brother Joe joined the Navy. As my dad and the whole family were proud, Dad decided that we would see him off to San Diego at the airport. So we all climbed into the Chevy, and off to the airport we went, my brothers explaining to me what was to happen.

Because I'm not the sharpest tool in the shed, it took me a little time to put into perspective the events that were occurring. And when we finally got to the gate, we said our good-byes, hugged, and Joe was off down the ramp that led to the plane. At that point, reality hit, and I started crying. Joe was gone. My dad asked me why I was crying, and I said that now, with Joe gone, I only had one brother.

Dad explained to me that, no, Joe may be gone, but he is still my brother, that I still had two brothers, that no matter what happened, I would always have my two brothers. Joe was a lot of things. Computer genius, ham radio operator, fly-fisher and ties his own flies, gardener, father to two amazing kids who truly he was proud of, Eagle scout, pony league baseball player, he worked at KPBS at Benson tech, clarinet player, electrician, I even saw him Morse dance once. But his greatest accomplishment was his marriage. He picked the perfect woman for him. Loved her with every ounce he had. And they have been married over forty years. When our dad wasn't doing so well in life after my mom passed away, even though he was still young, Joe helped Dad and took on some of the duties of the household. I remember when Joe was at Benson, he designed a hotdog cooker that used nails to cook the hotdog from the inside out using electricity. The one night we tried it, it was not pretty. Almost burned down the house and really stunk it up. Ever smell electrocuted meat? Dad never told him, but Dad was proud of him and appreciated all that Joe did for the family.

When Joe was going to Portland State, in the early years of computer science and after his enlistment in the Navy, Ross, my other brother, and I came home from school one day, and Joe was lying on the couch, kind of in an odd way. He was lying on his side, his arm was extended above him, and his hand was behind the bookcase. I think we surprised him, being home so early, and he was hiding something. We came to find out, it was a big bowl of ice cream—before dinner! Well, that was something! Joe being sneaky! Unheard of! But instead of being angry at us for discovering his sin, he invited us to share the bowl, and we sat on the couch, happily eating the treat before dinner. And I never saw him being sneaky again.

Joe was very much like Dad, and later in Dad's life, that's probably why they had disagreements, as Joe was taking over the leadership of the family. I could always tell when I wasn't doing the right thing with Joe. Like Dad, he would get that look on his face. He tried to hide it, but I knew . . . I knew. I may not have changed what I was doing, whether it be my choice of jobs or clothes or what have you, but at least I knew it was wrong, and in the end, I would usually modify my behavior to a more moderate state.

Joe was a family man to the nth degree. As I've said, he has two amazing daughters that he was very proud of and who have turned out to be a professional in both their careers and also in their families. Joe taught them well. Taught them to be old school in how they put their own families together. And now, they themselves are raising wonderful children and also having great careers, to boot. All this with me in the background, trying to corrupt them. When they were just barely teenagers, I bought them both makeup kits—big ones. Joe, to say the least, was not happy. But in the end, as with the ice cream, he gave in.

THE LOVE OF MY LIFE

Pat, Joe's wife, my sister-in-law, is an astounding person. I call her my sister proudly. She has been Mother Teresa through this whole ordeal. Not only did she make sure Joe made it to his doctors appointments, she has slogged through all the red tape of Social Security, beaten up nurses to get Joe fed, bathed, and treated well, and she has done the same for my other brother, Ross. If there is a heaven, Pat is going to be right up there at the head of the line, and watch out, St. Peter, she's a redhead with an attitude. She will kick your ass!

Alzheimer's is a son of a bitch. I hate it. I hate the name—it's too hard to spell. I hate that it has taken one of my brothers and is slowly taking the other. It has destroyed the family, made siblings into combatants, taken the soul of my brother's wife, to the point of nervous breakdown, and now, I have to stand up here and try to sum up the life of someone that has meant so much to so many people. I was always the rebel, the one who didn't do the good things, the one who ate poorly, took drugs, drank to excess, smoked whatever I could inhale, rode hard and fast on motorcycles, lived a life that should have ended well before my brothers, yet, Alzheimer's, you decided that my brothers were the ones . . . the ones whom you were going to make into shells . . . the ones who were the good ones. Why? Why the hell did you do that?

Well, Alzheimer's, you can't do that, not to me, not to my family, or the families of my brothers. Because after all is said and done, here in my heart and here in my mind and here in my soul, my brother might not be around, he might have left, but he is still my brother, and I will always have two brothers.

By Cortney

My father was loved by many. His kind heart and outgoing ways made him a joy to be around. Dad never seemed to get angry or cross, maybe a little disappointed now and then, but for the most part, he put himself out there, never a man to shy away. He even at times was so friendly that it would leave us high and dry for a bit! Be it helping the neighbors rather than getting his own household projects done. For example, the hole that was left in my mom's bathroom floor for *years* or introducing himself to the neighboring campsites, while us girls were still setting camp!

Dad suffered with Alzheimer's for eleven years. Some of the changes and stages were not always rapid, but some would catch you completely off guard. There were those moments of recognition too. When Dad would what Mom and I call have a spark! A moment of complete remembrance. Then it would be gone, like a flash of light. He, the Joe everyone knew and loved, was there again, and then it was gone!

With Alzheimer's, you have to learn to roll and laugh with the changes. Mom and I got good at laughing rather than getting upset. There was a time about six years ago when my mom had bought Dad a few new shirts. We asked him to go and try them on. After a few moments, we were wondering what was taking so long. My dad walked out of the bedroom with his shoulders up tight to his neck and arms in an awkward position. He had found Mom's new shirt and was trying to squeeze himself into it! Took us a little while to get him out due to the fact we were laughing too hard!

For the longest time, even after Dad entered the care center, Buddy and I would have my mom and dad over for Sunday dinner. One of the last times Dad came for dinner, we were having steak and, of course, red wine. Dad loved his red wine, and neither Mom, myself, nor Buddy thought much of how much may have been drinking.

We soon realized that each one of us kept filling his glass, because he was drinking it like cool aid! Well, us three got my dad stinking drunk, and we had to carry him to the car and back to the care center and tuck him in bed!

Many people use the excuse "I want to remember them as they were." Well, with Alzheimer's, life is ever changing, and even though the person reverts back to a younger form of their self, you still learn of who that person was. Stories you may not have known before that they are pleased to now tell you. Memories you can always capture before that person is gone for good

My dad's life was full of activities, love, and joy! He truly was a soulful man. He loved so many things, from animals, outdoor activities, his family and friends, and he was always trying and learning new things. I have learned so much from my dad, before he got ill and during the last several months. From being gracious, hardworking, and patient, even though *patience* is the hardest for me to learn! I will always be thankful for the love my dad showed me and taught me. Those are the memories I will keep, the memories Alzheimer's may have taken from my dad's mind but what Alzheimer's will never take from me.

Thank you.

By Morgan

Good afternoon

Please let me start off by saying thank you from the bottom of my heart to all of you for being here today. It's such a healing gift to be surrounded by your love and respect of my father. Thank you so much for coming and showing us that my dad holds a special place in your hearts too. Your friendship allows us to know that my father will be nearby always because of the memories stored within each of you.

When I first thought of the idea of speaking at Dad's funeral, I knew he would be honored, but I was terrified. What would I say? What if I left something out? I mean, how do you begin to thank someone whose first act to you was your very own existence and their unconditional love?

For days, month, and years, I've thought about what I could possibly say to bring honor to Dad in these moments. I could tell you loads and loads of information, but I really wanted to share more than just information on Dad's life. I hoped and prayed for the right words—eloquent and profound words to express what Dad meant to me. But all I have come up with is this:

I love being Daddy's little girl, a daddy's girl, Dad's baby girl, Joe's youngest. However you want to say it, I really, really, really loved being Dad's daughter.

Never will you meet a greater man, a man who more faithfully lived his values. My father was a teacher of all things. His methods were simple. He taught by example. At any age, when I had been faced with an ethical dilemma, after reflection, study, and even rationalization, I found myself coming back to one simple question, what would Dad do? Dad's character is the foundation of my conscience. He to this day and will always be my moral compass. He always wanted me to be a self-sufficient and independent woman. He wanted to make sure that our morals and values were aligned with his teachings, then the rest was up to us.

Speaking of my father's teachings—they really were endless. He taught me so many of my firsts. How to drive a manual car, how to thread a lure and cast a fishing rod, and how to gut and clean a fish. How to set up a tent, how to appreciate the outdoors. How to stick up for myself, and how to be kind, giving, loving, and loyal. The list goes on and on, but what this list made me realize was that my favorite childhood memories **all** involved dad.

At the risk of sounding clichéd, Dad was one of the greatest men I have ever known—and likely ever will. He was the most down-to-earth person you would ever meet. He just had a fundamental and abiding respect for all people. He immediately tried to see the best in everyone. Always!

But without a doubt, the most wonderful thing about my father was his humor. Especially at the most inopportune times. My father's one-liners were on rapid fire most of the time. His ability to come up with quick-witted responses never ceased to amaze me. My father could always make us laugh, even when we were mad and didn't want to. He could always cheer us up, and he had a beautiful way of making you see that you should never take life too seriously. I am so proud to say that this is one of the best lessons he has passed down to me. Life is too short to let anything or anyone make you unhappy.

My father had a quiet dignity, respecting himself the way he respected others. As he faced his illness, his mind failing, he always held on to his humor. My father's courage through his fight with Alzheimer's was incredible. We should all wish for one-tenth of the courage and the resolve that my father had. Even at the end of his life, Dad insisted that his brain be donated to research to aid in finding a cure for Alzheimer's.

I haven't quite come to terms with Dad's illness, his death, or the fact that I will never have another conversation with my dad again. I am sure I share that with many of you. The day Dad passed was the day we truly lost one of my greatest champions here on earth. I'm so grateful he was surrounded by our love and affection in his last days and moments.

Regardless of your beliefs in the afterlife, this much I can assure you: my father remains alive and well. He is all around me, in all of you, each and every day.

Thank you, Daddy, for being the most incredible father I could have ever wanted.

Thank you for making me want to make the world a better place and for showing me the path to do so. Thank you for making sure that I have known I was loved every single day of my life by you. You say you were lucky to have us in your life, but really, we were the lucky ones. Out of all the fathers in the world, you were given to us.

Daddy, I will miss you more than I can ever say. But I will love you forever, and I will always cherish being your daughter.

Joseph L. Michaud
April 30, 1947 to August 20, 2014

<u>Memorial Service</u>

Date: Wednesday August 27th, 2014

Time: 12:00 pm

Location:
Mt. Scott Funeral Home
4205 SE 59th Ave
Portland, OR 97206

Immediately following the funeral a police escort procession will take us up to:

Willamette National Cemetery for full Military Honor Commitment. 11800 SE Mt. Scott Blvd. 97086

Joseph L. Michaud
April 30, 1947 - Aug. 20, 2014

Joe Michaud's battle with Alzheimer's ended on August 20th, 2014 surrounded by friends and family. Joe is survived by his wife Patricia, daughters Courtney Turner and Morgan Anderson, his 5 grandchildren, 2 brothers and many loving extended family members.

Joe was an incredibly loving husband, father and grandfather and friend to all.

Joe will be missed by those who loved him and were blessed with his friendship.

Please sign the online guest book at www.oregonlive.com/obits

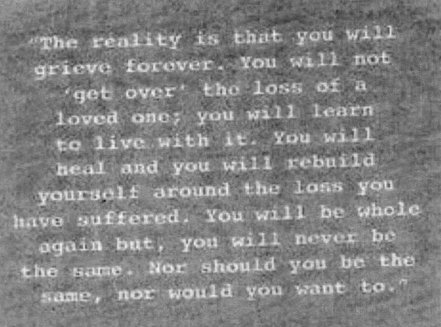

"The reality is that you will grieve forever. You will not 'get over' the loss of a loved one; you will learn to live with it. You will heal and you will rebuild yourself around the loss you have suffered. You will be whole again but, you will never be the same. Nor should you be the same, nor would you want to."

— Elizabeth Kubler-Ross and John Kessler

CHAPTER 15

Prayers and Poems That Comfort Me

The Lord's Prayer

The Lord is my shepherd, I shall not want,
he makes me lie down in green pastures.

He leads me beside still waters, he restores my soul,
he leads me in path of righteousness, for his name's sake.

Even though I walk through the valley of the shadow of death,
I fear no evil for thou art with me, thy rod and thy staff they
comfort me.

Thou prepares a table before me in the presence of my
enemies, thou anointed my head with oil, my cup overflows.

Surely goodness and mercy shall follow me all the days
of my life, and I shall dwell in the house of the Lord for ever.

—Psalm 23

PATRICIA MICHAUD

Our Father

Our Father who art in heaven, Hallowed be thy name.
Thy kingdom come, thy will be done,
on earth as it is in heaven.
Give us this day our daily bread.
And forgive us our debts, as we also have forgiven
our debtors.
And lead us not into temptation, but deliver us from evil.
For thine is the kingdom, and the power, and the glory, for ever.
Amen.

—Matthew 10:14

THE LOVE OF MY LIFE

Those we love
Don't go away,
they walk beside
us every day.

Unseen, unheard,
but always near.

So loved, so missed,
so very dear.

—Author unknown

PATRICIA MICHAUD

I still miss you as the days and years pass.
I still miss you as the pain of grief softens.
I still miss you as new memories are made.
I still miss you today and every day.
I still miss you.

—On Facebook

THE LOVE OF MY LIFE

The reality is that you will grieve forever.
You will not get over the loss of a loved one.
You will learn to live with it.
You will heal and you will rebuild yourself around the
loss you have suffered.
You will be whole again but you will never be the same.
Nor should you be the same, nor would you want to.

—Elizabeth Kubler Ross
and
John Kessler

PATRICIA MICHAUD

Do Not Ask Me to Remember

Do not ask me to remember, don't try to make me understand,
let me rest and know you're with me kiss
my check and hold my hand.

I'm confused beyond your concept, I am sad and sick and lost,
all I know is that I need you to be with me at all cost.

Do not lose your patience with me, do not scold or curse or cry,
I can't help the way I'm acting, can't be different though I try.

Just remember that I need you, that the best of me is gone,
please don't fail to stand beside me love me till my life is done.

—Author unknown

THE LOVE OF MY LIFE

Have no anxiety about anything, but in everything by prayer and supplication with thanksgiving, let your requests be made know to God.

—Philippians 4:6

PATRICIA MICHAUD

Why is it when we talk to God we are said to be praying, and when God talks to us we're said to be schizophrenic.

—Lily Tomlin

THE LOVE OF MY LIFE

I Am Free

Don't grieve for me, for now I'm free.
I'm following the path God laid for me,
I took his hand when I heard his call,
I turned my back, and left it all.
I could not stay another day.
To laugh, to love, to work or play,
Tasks left undone must stay the way,
I found that place at close of day.
If parting has left a void,
Then fill it with remembered joy,
A friendship shared, a laugh, a kiss,
ah yes, these things I too will miss.
Be not burdened with times of sorrow,
I wish for you the sunshine of tomorrow,
My life's been full, I savored much, good friends, good times,
a loved one's touch.
Perhaps my time seemed all too brief, don't lengthen
it now with undue grief.
Lift up your hearts, and share with me,
God wanted me now. He set me free.

—Author unknown

PATRICIA MICHAUD

If Heaven Had a Window

If heaven had a window and God granted me a view,
of all the beauty it beholds, I'd look for you.

I'd listen for your laughter that was always music to me, your
beautiful hair and hazel eyes is what I'd wish most to see.

If I could only view once more the smile that warmed my heart,
I'd treasure that moment as long as I live and we must be apart.

Here on earth I search for you and pray to God for signs,
and every day that passes you're still with me in my mind.

I know you're happy in heaven; you've earned your mansion indeed,
I imagine your kitchen table and you waiting there for me.

I love you and I miss you more than words can say, and
what I wouldn't give just to talk to you today.

I hope that you can hear me and listen to my thoughts, and
wherever this life takes me you know I've not forgot.

That once upon a time I was blessed and love, it's true
and if heaven had a window I'd only look for you.

—Kathy Parenteau

THE LOVE OF MY LIFE

To You Only

To live and love with you, and be one forever.

To be near you so I can reach out, and touch you.

To make love with you, laugh with you, cry with you,
talk with you and be silent with you.

To hold you close every night, waking up each morning.

To understand and respect you, accepting you for you.

To be with you through all the seasons, walking with you in
the sunshine and cuddling with in the cold.

To care for you when you are ill, and be joyful with you when
you are happy.

To grow old with you, and be with until the end of my time.
With you only, I want all these things for you only, I would do
all these things to you only, with all my love.

—Alberta Luciano

PATRICIA MICHAUD

An Alzheimer's Poem

Do not ask me to remember.
Don't try to make me understand.
Let me rest, and know you're with me.
Kiss my cheek, and hold my hand.
I'm confused beyond your concept.
I am sad and sick, and lost.
All I know is that I need you,
to be with me at all cost.
Do not lose your patience with me.
I can't help the way I'm acting.
Do not scold or curse or cry.
I can't be different though I try.
Just remember that I love and need you.
That the best of me is gone.
Please don't fail to stand beside me.
Always love me till my life is done.

—Author unknown

THE LOVE OF MY LIFE

He Only Takes the Best

A heart of gold stopped beating,
Hardworking hands now rest,
God broke our heart to prove to us,
He only takes the best.

We think of you in silence,
And often speak your name.
All we have now are memories,
And your pictures in a frame.

Many times we've missed you,
A million times we've cried.
If love alone could have saved you,
You never would have died.

It broke our hearts to lose you.
But you didn't go alone.
For a part of us went with you,
The day God took you home.

—Author unknown

PATRICIA MICHAUD

Footprints in the Sand

One night a man had a dream. He dreamed he was
walking along the beach with the LORD.
Across the sky flashed scenes from his life.
For each scene he noticed two
sets of footprints in the sand: one belong-
ing to him, and the other to the
LORD.

When the last scene of his life flashed
before him he looked back at the
footprints in the sand.

He noticed that many time along the path
his life there was only one set
of footprints.

Time of trial and suffering, when you see
only one set of footprints, it
he also noticed that it happened at the
very lowest and saddest time in
his life.

THE LOVE OF MY LIFE

This really bothered him and he questioned the LORD about it: "Lord you said that once I decided to follow you, you'd walk with me all the way. But I have noticed that during the most troublesome times in my life, there is only one set of footprints. I don't understand why when, I needed you most you would leave me." The LORD replied

"My son my precious child, I love you and I would never leave you. In your time of trial and suffering, when you see only one set of footprints that was when I carried you."

—Mark Stevenson

CHAPTER 16

What Helped Me Out

Books to Read for Awareness

1. *The Mayo Clinic for Alzheimer's*
2. *Alzheimer's for Dummy*
3. *36 Hours in a Day*
4. Books about Caregivers
5. *Caring for Those with Alzheimer's*
6. *Learning to Speak Alzheimer's*

I had a bereavement counselor with Gentiva Hospice by the name of Jack who helped me out a lot. He gave me some information, which he said I could use in my book, to help myself and others out there with it. It will help to understand the grieving process.

Also Providence Home Service has a pamphlet that will help you called "Seven Strategies: Coping with the Recent Death of a Loved One" presented by Providence Hospice Community Care Program.

The books I read to help me out are called as follows:

1. *How to Go On Living When Someone You Love Dies*
2. Therese A. Rando, PhD
3. *Second Firsts*
   Christina Rasmussen

About Care Facilities

American Association of Retired Persons
(AARP)
601 E. Street. NW
Washington, DC 20049
1-800-424-3410
www.aarp.org

Family Caregiver Alliance
180 Montgomery Street, Suite 1100
San Francisco, CA 94104
1-800-445-8106
www.caregiver.org

National Association of Area Agencies on Aging
1730 Rhode Island N.W, Suite 1200
Washington, DC 20036
1-202-872-0888
www.n4a.org

National Family Caregivers Association
10400 Connecticut Ave, Suite 500
Kensington, MD 20895
1-800896-3650
www.nfcares.org

U.S. Department of Health and Human
Services, Centers for Medicare and
Medicaid Services
7500 Security Blvd,
Baltimore, MD 21244-1850
1-800-633-4227
www.medicare.gov

Caregiving Skills

American Heart Association
7272 Greenville Avenue
Dallas, TX 75231
1-800-242-8721
www.americanheart.org

Family Caregiver Alliance
180 Montgomery Street, Suite 1100
San Francisco, CA 94104
1-800-445-8106

National Association for Home Care
228 Seventh Street, SE
Washington, DC 20003
1-202-547-7424

National Hospice and Palliative Care Organization
1700 Diagonal Road
Arlington, VA 22314
1-800-658-8898

Help in the Home

Resources:

American Association of Retired Persons
601 E. Street, NW
Washington, DC 20049
1-800-424-3410
www.aarp.org

Family Caregiver Alliance
180 Montgomery Street, Suite 1100
San Francisco. CA 94104
1-800-445-8106
www.caregiver.org

U.S. Dept. of Health and Human Services Centers for Medicare and Medicaid Services
7500 Security Boulevard
Baltimore, MD 21244
1-800-633-4227
www.medicare.gov

Helpful Websites

Administration on Aging
www.aoa.gov

American Diabetes Association
www.diabetes.org

Alzheimer's Association
www.alz.org

Alzheimer's Disease Education and Referral Center
www.alzheimers.org

Caregiving.com
www.caregiving.com

Eldercare Locator
www.eldercare.gov

Family Caregiver Alliance
www.caregiverg

Tools for Releasing Stress

1. Go for long walks
2. Walk in the morning
3. Listen to your favorite music
4. Read a good book
5. Play with your grandkids
6. Go browse in the stores
7. Play games, card games
8. Clean your car with a friend
9. Just meditate
10. Take a hot bath
11. Spend time with your family and friends
12. Dance and laugh
13. Go outdoors or to the beach
14. Have a good cry or just scream
15. Have a glass of wine or two
16. Go to the movies

CHAPTER 17

A Recap

I hope you enjoyed reading this book. I also hope it did not scare you too much. I just wanted to let you know about the love of my life. I enjoyed sharing it with you. We had such a great and happy life together. This was a very difficult and hard thing to go through, with all the memories we had shared together, also to recall all of them. If this book can help you in any way, for you or for a loved one to understand the hardship that this disease called Alzheimer's can bring on. For the whole family, not just the person that was diagnosed with Alzheimer's, but how it will tear a whole family apart right to the core of your being. You will definitely see what family and friends are made of with this disease. It will also show you all the good times, along with the bad ones ahead of you.

Please also know that this is one of God's test for all of us. He had it in store for me and my family from the beginning. I know I shouldn't look back on all the bad parts, but I do, and I know that it is what is making me strong. I just rejoice with all the great times Joe and I had together, with all the loving memories that we shared. I have learned so much about what this disease can do to all of us, so I know you will be able to do it also. I hope this is helpful to you and gives you some comfort in the knowledge of what may lie ahead of you and your family. To survive and be able to look forward, with all your old memories tucked away safely in your heart and soul for safekeeping. And to know you are not alone along this journey.

You will have all the knowledge of being loved in your past with you, but also know that there is a new and different life waiting for you to start when you are ready.

As of today, Ross is doing quite well in cottage 1. The only two words he will speak is "Thank you." His health is great, and we are all thankful for that one. Tony and I go to see him all the time, which makes him happy and us happy to. We get into big arguments and discussions just to make him laugh.

About the Author

Pat was born and raised in Portland, Oregon, with two sisters and one brother. She lived in the same house until she met and married Joe. Today, she lives in the house where Joe and she raised their two daughters. She is blessed with five grandchildren. She shares the house now with her golden retriever, Reno.

She enjoys volunteering at her grandsons' school or helping with their sport activities. Her other interests are gardening, hiking, and playing golf. She belongs to a local Red Hat Society chapter and enjoys the friendship of these ladies. She holds a ham radio technician license.

www.ingramcontent.com/pod-product-compliance
Lightning Source LLC
Chambersburg PA
CBHW060400080526
44583CB00012B/401